AF530970

Rita Deanin Abbey RIO GRANDE SERIES

To my husband, Robert,

who shares my vision

and understands my prayers

for the environment

Rita Deanin Abbey

Marc Simmons

Katherine Plake Hough

William L. Fox

Gan Or Las Vegas, Nevada

Rita Deanin Abbey **RIO GRANDE SERIES**

Rita Deanin Abbey **RIO GRANDE SERIES**

Published by Gan Or
P.O. Box 35653
Las Vegas, Nevada 89133

Poems by Rita Deanin Abbey, Las Vegas
Photographs of the art by Gregory Preston, Las Vegas
Photo of the artist by Kerry, Las Vegas
Design by Lilli Colton, Los Angeles

Type composed in Cochin and Copperplate
First edition
Printed in Hong Kong

Front cover: *Rio Grande Series #2*
Back cover: *Rio Grande Series #25*

Library of Congress Cataloging-in-Publication Data

Abbey, Rita Deanin.
Rio Grande series/Rita Deanin Abbey: [essays by] Marc Simmons. Katherine Plake Hough: [foreword by] William L. Fox.
p. cm.
ISBN 0-9652870-0-9
1. Abbey, Rita Deanin—Themes, motives. 2. Rio Grande in art.
I. Simmons, Marc. II. Hough, Katherine Plake. III. Title.
NE2246.A22A4 1996
769.92—dc20 96-23835
CIP

CONTENTS

8 Acknowledgments

9 Foreword *William L. Fox*

11 Rio Grande *Marc Simmons*

19 Rio Grande Series *Katherine Plake Hough*

23 The Space Between The Forms *Rita Deanin Abbey*

25 Artist's Statement

27 The Genesis Of My Awareness *Rita Deanin Abbey*

29 Rio Grande Series

95 Artist's Biography

My deepest appreciation to:

Robert Rock Belliveau

Marc Simmons

Katherine Plake Hough

William L. Fox

Aaron Paul Abbey

Foreword

William L. Fox

"To abstract" means to draw from, and away from, a particular instance, to get at essential form apart from pictorial representation. The desert lends itself to abstraction, appearing to us as if the flesh of the land had been drawn away and the intrinsic bones of the earth revealed.

Rita Deanin Abbey, who has worked extensively and lived in the American Southwest since 1950, is an artist deeply schooled in traditional methods as well as in contemporary abstraction. She is very much of "place" in general, and the desert in particular; it is rare that the impetus for her work strays too far from the spirit of the land. The mixed media monotypes of the *Rio Grande Series* constitute one among many discrete subsets of her work which are successfully grounded upon, yet abstracted from, her close observation of the desert, an accomplishment notable in many of her works based on geological features.

Executed in 1987 and dealing with one of the great desert rivers in the Southwest, the *Rio Grande Series* is the dynamic evocation of a specific and powerful presence. As the eminent author and historian Marc Simmons points out in his essay, the nearly 2,000 mile-long Rio Grande and its central basin in New Mexico are "at the heart of the Southwest and are the focus of a complex interplay of natural and human forces that entrance geologists, archeologists, historians, artists, and poets." Abbey has evinced the complex nature of the river in her monotypes as a vivid force cutting gorges through the Colorado Plateau while animating the plains of the region. It's a cold wet source in a hot dry climate, a smooth surface with a turbulent under flow.

Katherine Plake Hough, Director of Collections and Exhibitions at the Palm Springs Desert Museum, noted in her catalog essay accompanying Abbey's thirty-five year retrospective exhibition in 1988 that the artist "experienced the line, pattern, color, space, light, form, and texture of geological formations," which enabled her to "recreate the spirit and essence of the desert in abstract compositions." And as she writes here: "With forms and surfaces suggestive of geological processes and, therefore, time, her monotypes acquire a sense of the Rio Grande's movement and changing contours."

Whether in printmaking or casting bronze sculptures, Abbey makes exact and exuberant one-of-a-kind works in media conventionally meant for multiples. Hough points out another polarity: "The desert, simultaneously empty and full, is the traditional geography of revelation." Abbey thus creates and plays within numerous such tensions: traditional methods fused with contemporary abstraction; singular images accumulating in series; and the figure of water in an "empty" desert. It's a dangerous strategy, attempting to reconcile so many opposing factors, but in risking it she achieves a compositional harmony that cohabits both place and art. We should be grateful for these works that are gathered together in this book and thereby draw us toward a deeper sense of where we are. ■

Santa Fe, NM

William L. Fox is a poet and arts writer who is completing a book on art and artists in the Great Basin. He is the former executive director of the Nevada State Council on the Arts.

RIO GRANDE

Marc Simmons

High upon the cold and wind-blasted eastern slope of Colorado's Continental Divide, rivulets of snowmelt and spring water flow together, giving birth to one of America's mighty rivers, the Rio Grande. After winding eastward through the coniferous forests of the high country, it drops serenely into the pancake flat San Luis Valley. In the vicinity of Alamosa, the river makes a sweeping bend toward the south and points its course in the direction of New Mexico.

By the time it crosses the Colorado line, the Rio Grande is well into its erosional work of cutting down through the earth's crust to form an eye-stunning gorge that near Taos reaches a depth of more than 1,000 feet. Known locally as The Box, this gorge with foamy water tumbling over massive boulders remains true wilderness, protected now by the National Wild and Scenic Rivers Act. Southwest of Taos, an old and fabled town, the river breaks free of the uplands and continues its descent through a series of elliptical valleys, each one strung along the silvery water course like beads on a necklace. These valleys, furnished with fertile if narrow floodplains, all take their Spanish names from principal towns within: Española, Santo Domingo, Albuquerque, Belen, Socorro, Mesilla, and finally El Paso.

After parting New Mexico down its center, the Rio Grande near the upper end of the El Paso Valley commences to serve as the international boundary between Texas and Mexico. The direction of flow from this point forward is sharply southeastward, except where the river makes a spectacular looping curve, called the Big Bend, above its junction with the Pecos. After rolling past sandy plains studded with thorny mesquite and prickly pear, the Rio Grande threads its way through palmetto marshes to empty into the Gulf of Mexico, almost 2,000 miles from its point of origin in the Colorado mountains.

The central portion of the Rio Grande and its attenuated basin stretching from northern New Mexico down to El Paso lie at the heart of the Southwest and are the focus of a complex interplay of natural and human forces that entrance geologists, archeologists, historians, artists, and poets. Albuquerque-born novelist Harvey Fergusson once remarked that the river's middle valley has fed generations of people, offered them a main route of travel, and provided a congenial setting for homes. "It is a place," said he, "where journeys and migrations began and ended, where battles were fought and destinies decided." It persists also as a refuge for the romantic imagination, he concluded.

The formal story of the upper Rio Grande was initiated by Europeans who began keeping a written historical record more than 400 years ago. When Spaniards under

Francisco Vásquez de Coronado first entered its valley in September of 1540, they heard the river called P'osoge by the resident Pueblo Indians, which in their language meant Great River. The main stream channel then was much wider and deeper than it is today, and as there existed no other river anywhere close by that could rival it, in either size or volume, the name seemed quite apt. For Coronado's men, however, P'osoge proved too strange and heathen-sounding for their tastes, so they christened it El Rio de Nuestra Señora, or The River of Our Lady.

But that name did not last. A Franciscan padre in 1581 proposed calling it Guadalquivir, after the foremost river in southern Spain. Yet, it too, after a brief period of popularity, fell by the wayside. Later through common usage, Rio Grande del Norte emerged as the favored and accepted name — the Great River of the North. So, Great River it was to be after all, just as the Pueblos had initially decided.

The problem was that in spite of its importance as a valued water source in a semi-arid land, the Rio Grande could scarcely be counted as a great river in anything but its length. Stacked against the Mississippi, the Missouri, the Columbia, or any one of a dozen other major American rivers that run broad and deep, the Rio Grande makes a poor showing. Indeed, there are times when drought and irrigation leave its channel dry. Humorist Will Rogers once visited the middle valley in late summer and found that the water in the Rio Grande had disappeared.

"Why friend," he told his tour host Governor Clyde Tingley, "you ought to be out there right now irrigatin' that river to keep it from blowin' away."

In terms of greatness, if the Rio Grande comes off poorly by comparison, some compensation can be found in its rich history and in the impact the river has long had upon the development of regional cultures. The tale has its beginnings some 10,000 years ago when ancient inhabitants, known as Folsom man, hunted bison in the grasslands bracketing the valley. These people eventually vanished to be succeeded by seed gatherers, and they in turn by true farmers who were also architects and builders of multistoried adobe towns, or *pueblos,* as Spaniards termed them.

Coronado was astonished by the prosperity of the Pueblo Indians in their river kingdom and by their material progress. A Spanish explorer who followed later remarked: "They are the most domestic and industrious people, and the best craftsmen found in New Spain." The Pueblos have always lived in a world of mysticism and symbolism, a world in which supernaturalism joins man to his natural environment. As agriculturalists dependent upon rain and the river, their abiding concern was with cycles of weather and crop fertility. Native belief rested upon the interrelatedness of sacred and worldly matters, so that the Rio Grande in Pueblo eyes was not just a natural resource to be exploited, but rather an essential element in their cosmos deserving of reverence and awe.

The coming of the Spaniards marked a watershed in the long history of New Mexico's Indian people and in the story of the Rio Grande itself. After centuries of comparative isolation, the Pueblos were now drawn into close and irritating contact with Europeans, whose alien ways and beliefs would upset the old familiar pattern of native life. Spanish governors and missionaries, regarding themselves as chosen servants of God and the king, set out to reshape the Indian, for his own good, in the image prescribed by Hispanic society and religion. These conceits bore bitter fruit, notably in 1680 when the Pueblos rose in bloody revolt. Surviving settlers and friars fled down the Rio Grande to the El Paso Valley where they huddled in exile until the reconquest twelve years later.

Colonists, both before and after the great revolt, gravitated to the Rio Grande and its slender tributaries, like the Chama, Nambé, Tesuque, Galisteo, Jemez, Puerco, and Salado. They needed a permanent flow of water to tap for irrigation and to turn their cumbersome tub mills for grinding grain. Further, the alluvial soil in the valleys was highly fertile and produced bountifully when put to the ox-drawn plow. In part that was owing to the tendency of the Rio Grande to overflow its banks during the spring snowmelt and deposit a rich burden of silt on cropland, one-quarter inch or more yearly.

In 1832 Antonio Barreiro, a Santa Fe attorney, referred to the Rio Grande as "this voluminous Nile, the soul of the Territory." And a century before, one Franciscan padre had exclaimed exuberantly: "The great Rio del Norte is a beautiful image of the celebrated Nile." Likening the annual flood waters of the Rio Grande to those of the Egyptian Nile was perhaps a natural comparison, one drawn as well by incoming nineteenth century Anglo-Americans. They also noted the Nile-like quality of another prominent Southwestern river, the Colorado, in its last hundred miles or so before emptying into the Sea of Cortez.

Rio Grande water was a soil restorer by another means, too. A Vermont journalist, visiting New Mexico in 1881, wrote: "Irrigation is a fertilizer of itself." By that he meant that water from irrigation ditches spreading across the surface of fields released mineral-laden silt which served, in the phrasing of the time, as "manure for the land." In effect, therefore, the farmlands of the Rio Grande Valley were auto-replenishing. The silt provided another benefit, as well. It coated the sides and bottom of the ditches, or *acequias*, helping to cut down on seepage and thereby conserving water.

In another way, the river contributed to the support and pleasure of Indian and Spaniard alike — it nourished the *bosques*, the groves of Rio Grande cottonwood. Now, as then, in summer their dense green foliage spreads a welcome lattice of shade upon the channel's banks, and in autumn they become a blaze of gold. Spanish colonists found the cottonwood to be a splendid resource. The wood, lightweight, long-fibered, and soft but tough, provided fence posts, corral poles, timber for architectural purposes, and material for a variety of agricultural and domestic implements, including carts, plow beams, and kitchen utensils. Cottonwood also makes a good fuel. Even today Pueblo Indians on the river like to burn it because it produces a hot fire and leaves little ash.

While cottonwoods are predominant in the middle Rio Grande Valley, other varieties of trees can be found. Willows, particularly shrub types, grow thickly in boggy places along the shores. At present they are interspersed with two ornamental trees that escaped from cultivation within the last century and spread throughout the Southwest's waterways: the Russian olive, with narrow, silver-backed leaves, and the tamarisk, also known as salt cedar, which has thin wiry branches adorned with feathery leafage and clusters of tiny pink flowers in season.

All of these trees provide nesting for doves and songbirds and cover for terrestrial wildlife. They also stabilize the river banks during flooding and shield the levees from erosion and scouring. The same benefits are offered by stands of cattails, rushes, and sedges and by salt grass and horseweed, which form the vegetation under the shading trees.

Just as the encroachment of man over the past several centuries has restricted and changed the flora, so too has it affected the habitat of small mammals and birds. Draining of marsh and overflow ponds, conversion of land to agriculture or housing subdivisions, and expanded use of herbicides and pesticides take their toll. Rodent control measures, for example, have all but eliminated colonies of prairie dogs that once pocked the alluvial plain and lateral mesas.

Though in retreat, wild creatures nevertheless survive in surprising numbers, mainly in the sheltered areas inside the levees. Beavers and muskrats can be found on the river and along irrigation ditches where they make burrows in the banks. Raccoons, weasels, skunks, porcupines, squirrels, cottontails, and pocket gophers have all managed to establish an uneasy equilibrium between themselves and man. But they fall constant prey to guns, traps, poison, and, when crossing city streets or highways, to automobiles.

Many of the 400 species of resident and migratory birds recorded in the Southwest can be observed seasonally amid the *bosques*. When George W. Kendall passed down the valley in 1841, he took note of "immense flocks of blue and white herons and wild geese ... exceedingly tame." The Spanish folk only occasionally hunted the river bottom for ducks and geese, and then not to a degree that it ever made a dent in their numbers.

During the last quarter of the nineteenth century, when the killing of birds became a national pastime and a national disgrace, the Rio Grande Valley's winged creatures seem to have escaped decimation only because the Anglo population remained relatively small. Harvey Fergusson, who as a boy at the turn of the century whiled away many an hour, alone or with chums, stalking birds in the fields and marshes that impinged on the river, recalled years afterward that wild fowl abounded. In cloudlike swarms, they darkened the sky during spring and fall migrations.

"I will never forget," Fergusson relates, "the first wild mallard drake I killed when I was about ten, with his plush-green head, the rich chestnut of his breast, and the iridescent purple of his wing-bars. He was beautiful as a jewel or a flower and I was proud of him as though I had created rather than killed him."

Through its gifts of precious moisture and useful sediment and through its park-like *bosques* and colonies of wildlife, the Rio Grande appears friendly to humankind. But it has another side, a menacing one as history shows. In periods of flood, it can become an angry torrent with cresting waves that devour the low banks, reroute the channel, and destroy man's buildings, diversion dams, headgates, and ditches. The high water, often instead of spreading slowly and evenly as it did on the Egyptian plain, would sweep down, in the words of a U. S. Army surgeon in 1852, "with a force that undermines and ruins hundred of acres of cultivated land in a single season and forms extensive deposits with incredible rapidity." Nor were all the deposits he mentions, the desired silt. Gravels and sterile sands sometimes formed in shoals and when waters receded were found to overlay once prosperous fields.

Father Alonso de Benavides, as early as 1634, speaks of the inconvenience caused by bad flooding. Indeed, the problem seems to have reached far back into prehistoric times. Adolph Bandelier, after witnessing a devastating flood in 1884 that inundated almost 200 miles of New Mexico's middle valley, speculated that the phenomenon helped explain many aspects of the early Indian occupation and abandonment of the country.

"It shows," he said, "that the Rio Grande bottom, perfectly habitable and safe during long periods of time, may suddenly be swept by a flood obliterating in many places human habitation, and burrowing new channels, thus permanently changing the distribution of arable plots and sites for pueblos." Just two years after Bandelier wrote, flood waters destroyed the fields of Santo Domingo Pueblo and much of the village itself.

The river proved malevolent in other ways. It has few natural fords, and in the old days when men, livestock, and wagons were obliged to cross, they sometimes fell victim to quicksands. The Pueblos constructed simple foot bridges by planting forked beams at intervals in the muddy bottom and spanning them with squared timbers. The Spaniards repeatedly built bridges wide enough for vehicles, but in every case they were washed away with the rise of the spring freshets.

The colonial New Mexicans, in their own fashion, learned to live with the capricious river, accepting with gratitude what it bestowed but also accepting with resignation the hardships that it imposed. The Anglo Americans, however, after their arrival in the nineteenth century, were a different matter. They regarded the Rio Grande as something to be harnessed, controlled, manipulated. Their man-made levees and dams held back the flood waters and regulated the current's flow. That allowed house building and farming on certain lands that formerly had been unusable. Yet, new problems were created. The river, confined, no longer spread over the valley at flood stage dropping its fertilizing silt. Indeed, there was no longer much silt to deposit, the upstream dams having trapped and impounded it. Behind the dams, the riverbed began to aggrade, its progressive rising occasioned by the slowing of the current which resulted in deposition of sediment. That caused neighboring fields to become waterlogged and useless for agriculture.

New systems of riverside drains and diversion dams together with heavy use of domestic and industrial wells caused a lowering of the water table in areas of concentrated population such as Albuquerque and El Paso. The decline of wetlands followed and, in fact, New Mexico has lost roughly half of its riparian areas since the advent of Anglo settlement. Human crowding along the river has also contributed to increased contamination through discharge of wastewater containing, among other pollutants, mercury, and low level radioactive material. The health of the Rio Grande, of course, is a handy bellwether of the health of the surrounding environment. The degradation of the river is thus more than of incidental concern.

The Rio Grande occupies its own special niche in an enormous Southwestern landscape. The river as it once was is now gone, and in its place is a new and different river. Over time it has been painted and photographed and written about by way of providing something of an interpretive record. But at bottom, the Rio Grande remains itself — sublime, ageless, a kind of eternal monument to nature with its own inanimate rhythm of existence. In tracing its way from the heights of Colorado to the lowlands of the Mexican gulf, the Rio Grande still retains the capacity to make history. ■
Cerrillos, NM

Marc Simmons, Ph.D., is a professional historian and author of the Southwest. His writings, lectures, and research focus on the Indian and Hispanic heritages of New Mexico. Dr. Simmons received his higher education at the University of Texas, University of New Mexico, and the University of Guanajuato (Mexico). His writings include thirty-five books, more than one hundred articles in scholarly and popular journals, and a weekly history column appearing in several newspapers. Dr. Simmons is a former Woodrow Wilson Fellow and recipient of a Guggenheim Fellowship to carry out a study of Hispanic agriculture in New Mexico. He was knighted by order of the King of Spain in 1993 for his contributions to Spanish colonial history of the Southwest.

Katherine Plake Hough

For over forty-six years the allure of the American Southwest landscape has had a major influence on Rita Deanin Abbey's work. Experimenting with diverse media and using nature as a point of departure, she has created images based on her visual perceptions and subjective impressions of the desert environment — geological formations of massive mountains, deep canyons, varicolored arroyos, rugged rivers, and changing atmospheric conditions of light, clouds, storms, and rain. In turn, these images suggest mysteries of the desert's spirit and essence in abstract compositions that accentuate movement and tension.

The spirit of these places flows throughout Abbey's works. She makes sense of the desert phenomena through visual metaphors that link her experiences, fortifying nonobjective compositions with geological information. Abbey works from the inside, arriving at images from emotional instincts that overlay personal memory onto historical and geological fact.

In the process of filling her work with desert-linked images and forms, Abbey has discovered personal definitions of and relationships to abstraction. Her intent is not to imitate nature but to present ideas in which she identifies forms in nature with those resulting from the creative process. For her, the cumulative effects of the desert landscape translate her thoughts into images and her images into thoughts.

In the *Rio Grande Series* of 1987, consisting of 32 mixed media monotypes on paper, Abbey has continued her exploration of color, movement, and the interaction of organic and geometric nonobjective elements of composition. Working without a master printer and without a press at the University of New Mexico's Tamarind Institute, Abbey was engulfed in the creative process as she hand printed the series. She applied oil-based inks to a 1/4 inch Lexan plate and pressed damp paper over the image. She then burnished the back of the paper with a baren, a tool she acquired during her study of the woodcut with Toshi Yoshida in Japan. Her free execution is evident in the spontaneous style. Later she enhanced individual works by using drawn lines to function as bridges between colors and planes in oil pastel, oil-based ink, and graphite. Some works were collaged with Japanese papers of varying weights and textures, which were used to emphasize shape and cause areas to recede and merge in subdued light. This atmospheric effect alters mood and contrasts with areas of vivid color and activated line. Abbey used experimental printing techniques to develop innovative images.

The Tamarind Institute has a long history of inviting artists and printers to collaborate in the creative process. In the 1940s American painters discovered that making prints was an artistically justified, often rewarding, and gratifying outlet for their creative energy. With the revival of hand lithography in the late 1950s, the medium became available to many artists who provided the vital imagery that started the print boom of the past three decades. On several occasions Abbey executed lithographs, monoprints, and monotypes at Tamarind. She was commissioned by the Palm Springs Desert Museum to produce a four-color lithograph to commemorate its fiftieth anniversary in 1988.

By manipulation of traditional printing processes in the *Rio Grande Series,* Abbey has radically altered customary relationships between the printed image and its support, incorporating unprinted margins into the spatial integrity of the work. Abbey seeks tangible references to prevailing spatial elements — the edges and negative space of the printing paper, which she integrates into a forceful illusion of three-dimensionality. Definition of space is a consistent subject for intense study. The act of transforming the constantly changing "river" or flow of creative energy is a functional element of the work and her processes. The real interest of this work lies in the quality of its expression rather than in the technical means by which its expression is realized.

In the monotypes of the *Rio Grande Series,* as in the watercolors of the *Rivertrip Series* of 1971–1972, Abbey's emotional responses to the rivers are recorded in highly expressive works. Small in format (unlike her paintings and sculptures), both series are executed with spontaneous gestures packed with explosive personal treatment of layered color, line, and texture. Abbey has successfully captured the spirit of the rivers by contrasting organic textures with geometric shapes and vital color.

With forms and surfaces suggestive of geological processes and, therefore, time, her monotypes acquire a sense of the Rio Grande's movement and changing contours. Abbey has continued to intuitively develop compositional elements to discover and reveal images. Her emotional and expressive use of form and color are grounded by an underlying structure that refers to topography. Tensions produced by fragmented segments are resolved and unified, creating a strong three-dimensional illusion. The perceived feeling of geological time is imbued with nature's harmony and balance.

In many of the monotypes, line drawing is central either in the form of the color area contours or in larger units of printed and drawn color. The handling of line reveals the artist's concern for preserving something of traditional imagery within her purely abstract framework. In these works, however, printing and drawing are often separated and counterposed. The contours of the color areas read as though they are drawn.

The separation and ambiguity that appear enhance the energy of a new vision. They both join and hold apart broad planes of color that intensify dynamic relationships. In the *Rio Grande Series #15* and *#16,* the line drawing is deliberately interwoven with the contour of emerging forms. In *#3* abrupt color accents appear that are neither elements of line drawing nor color areas, although they function simultaneously as both. The line drawing is not so much a framework for color as a way of moving, modulating, and drawing color. In such works as *#1* and *#2,* the line seems set into the framework of color areas to define textures and planes. Dark and light contrasts in *#6* are led by electric lines into the heart and mystery of the composition. In *#7* the line drawing is embedded into the areas of color, yet the diagonal movement of the line is in opposition to the direction of the planes. The spare composition of *#18* announces color with extraordinary authority and independence. The separate, parallel, and straight black lines connect the two zones on a single plane that would otherwise separate. In *#24* something explosive under the surface threatens to fragment the textured areas, but overlapping planes integrate and hold them together. Light and dark are divided in *#27,* juxtaposing broad linear strokes in positive and negative space. All nearly square in shape, the majority of these mixed media monotypes use line drawing to span their forms and temper the geometry of the spatial structure. Regardless of these and other variations, dynamic color remains a discrete component in this body of work.

Forms in nature hold a basic fascination for Abbey, confirming personal bonds with the earth. The desert, simultaneously empty and full, is the traditional geography of revelation. Abbey's work develops from this diversity and continues in a creative and steady stream of change with new waters rushing in, like the rivers that compel her. ■
Palm Springs, CA

Katherine Plake Hough received a Bachelor of Arts degree from California State University, Long Beach, and a Master of Arts degree in museum studies and exhibition design from California State University, Fullerton. She began her museum career in 1975 as Registrar at the Palm Springs Desert Museum. In 1979 she became the Curator of Art, and since 1995 has served as the Director of Collections and Exhibitions. During her twenty-one year career at the Palm Springs Desert Museum, Hough has authored twenty-seven exhibition catalogs and numerous articles on American art. She has organized thirty-three exhibitions, including nine that have traveled.

The Space Between The Forms

I, finite and thick,

A silent speck of matter,

Search the shapes and colors

For understanding.

Momentarily,

With the obstacle of myself removed,

Sensations of life

Beyond my thoughts

From unseen vision

Become

The gnarled fragrant cedar,

The fading outline at dusk,

The space between the forms.

Rita Deanin Abbey

In 1987 I worked on large lithographs and monoprints at the University of New Mexico's Tamarind Institute in Albuquerque, New Mexico. After the presses shut down in the late afternoon, I hand printed monotypes which I then expanded with mixed media. These works grew into the Rio Grande Series.

During that particular residency at Tamarind and others since then, I had occasion to walk along the Rio Grande River, reminisce, and search for old sites where I sketched in the early 1950s when I was a student at the University of New Mexico. The inspiration I derived from the magic of the river's changing light, colors, textures, and hypnotic motion was still clearly in focus. I recalled bolting down the hill from campus on my bicycle, with my sketchbook and drawing materials tied to the back wheel rack of my bike, excitedly anticipating the hours I would spend by the river. In the midst of the surprises and nuances I found in nature, I drew fervently, and explored my inner self and the surroundings. The Rio Grande's seductive rhythm often carried me in its flow, and I envisioned the people and land along its meandering course, and its contoured, eroding boundaries. I imagined myself as an organic particle of matter in the current, traveling from the river's source, dissolving and disappearing into the Gulf of Mexico.

My nostalgia for student days, magnified by memories of sketching in the Rio Grande gorge where I took my sons, Joshua and Aaron, when we lived in Taos, made lasting impressions that contributed to the imagery of the Rio Grande Series.

I have been attracted to other rivers — the Payette's turbulent white water in Idaho and the Virgin River's diversity of form in Utah and Nevada. I have taken raft trips on the Middle Fork of the Salmon in Idaho, the Green in Utah, the Roaring Fork in Colorado, and the Nenana, the Eagle, and the Kenai Rivers in Alaska. My first and longest raft trip, through Cataract Canyon, enabled me to become acquainted with the Colorado River, the geology of its canyon walls, and its plants and wildlife. The distinctive characteristics of each river have touched my life and work, but when I am in New Mexico along the Rio Grande, I am home.

The swift passage of the last forty six years remains an enigma. Since I first explored the Rio Grande, time has unfolded like the course of a river accelerating with its own complex destiny. The body of my work, the product of these years, exposes my need to experiment with diverse media and reveals a creative struggle along an intuitive and emotional course. I continue to seek ways to challenge myself and express the essential harmonious relationships that I observe in nature.

What I instinctively felt by the Rio Grande in my youth, and slowly learned as I grew older, was that the meandering river carved and defined its embankments within limitations, subject to the forces acting upon it. Harsh weather, erosion, and gravity are inescapable realities, as are the given realities of our own nature. Yet there are ways in which to grow and develop, and ways to understand and appreciate earth's gifts.

The Rio Grande Series *is a perception of what is out there and in my heart. I know I will never be able to explain creative impulse and process, but I will continue, as long as I can, to search for a route that unlocks my imagination and deeper feelings. I look to nature for insights into myself and the way things fundamentally work and come together.* ■
Las Vegas, NV

The Genesis of My Awareness

My small friend the spider
Joins the stone I am holding,
Then my hand.
The sun warms us together
And we are home in a place
Immediate and lasting.

It's a green day
As filmy veils blur the edges
And light creeps into unexpected spaces,
Pulling purple into darkened crevices,
Reminding me of unseen cells,
Of mysterious forms within
The abstract power of life … and death
In the larger dimension.

My eye is a servant
Obeying this world of shadows,
Seeking permanence amidst change,
Seeking the symmetry of essence.

Nature's eye is its own.

Rita Deanin Abbey RIO GRANDE SERIES, 1987

Rio Grande Series #1

Mixed media monotype on Rives BFK paper
13 1/4 x 15 1/4 inches

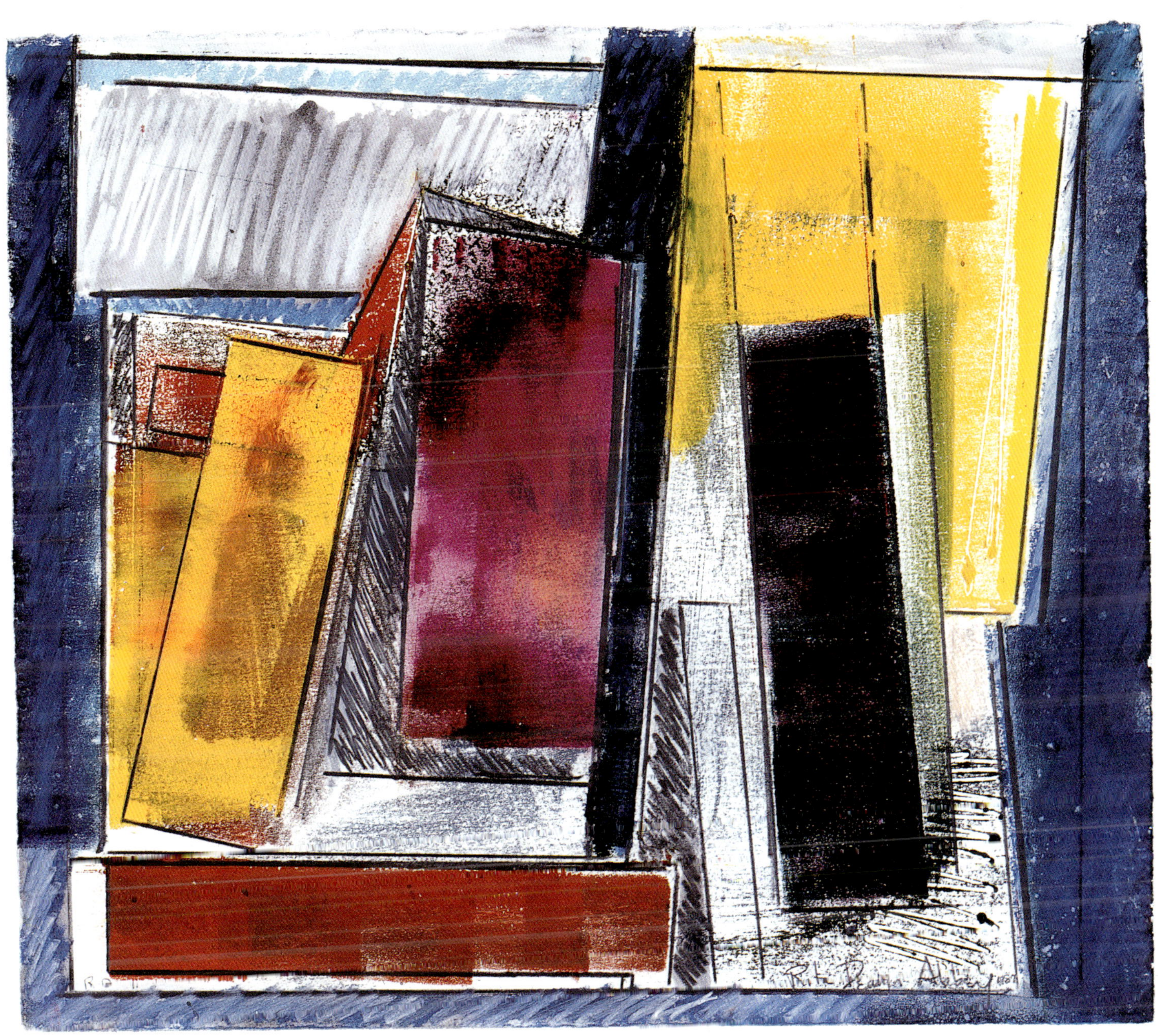

Rio Grande Series #2

Mixed media monotype on Rives BFK paper
15 x 13 1/4 inches

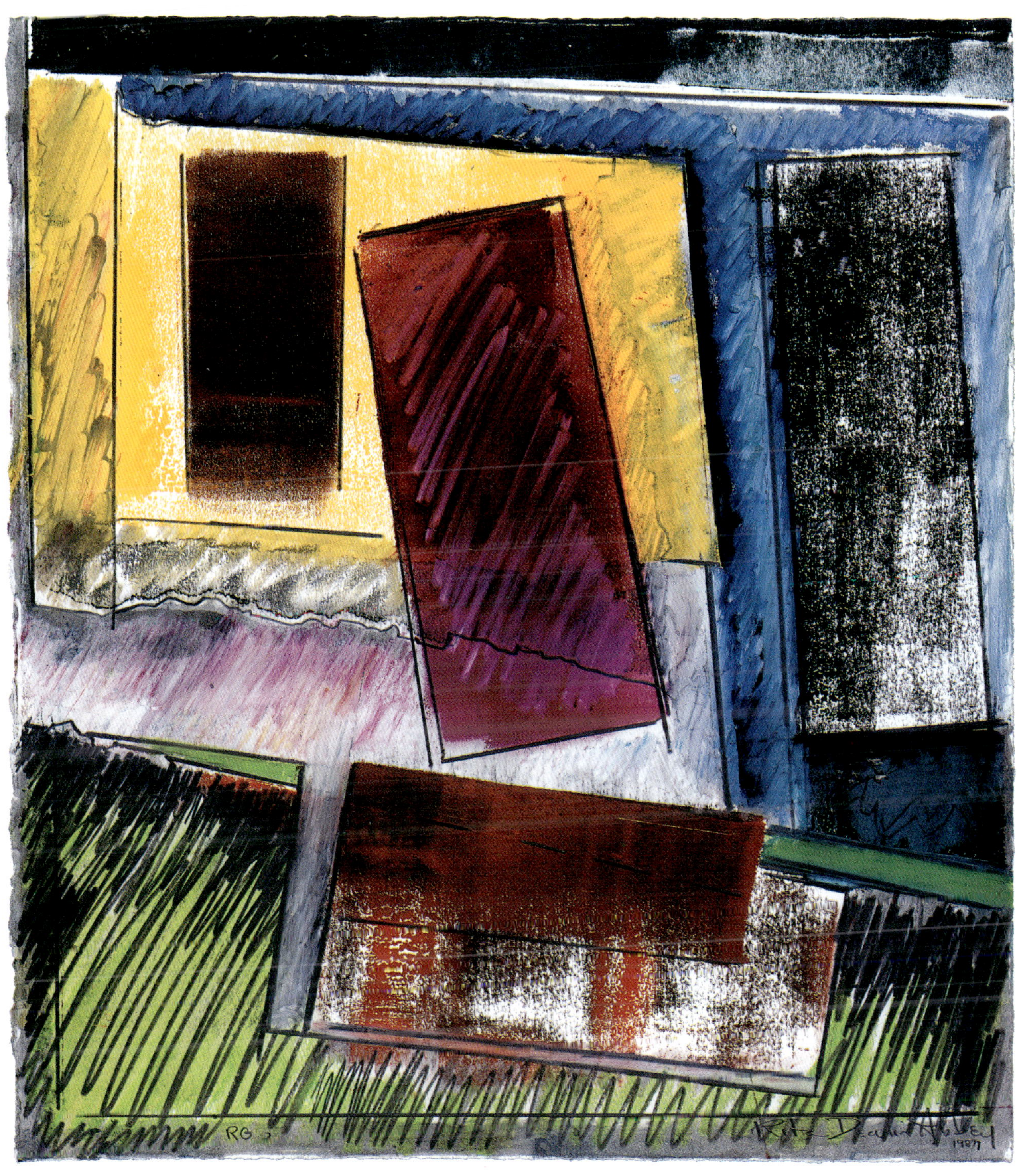

Rio Grande Series #3

Mixed media monotype on Rives BFK paper
13 1/4 x 15 inches

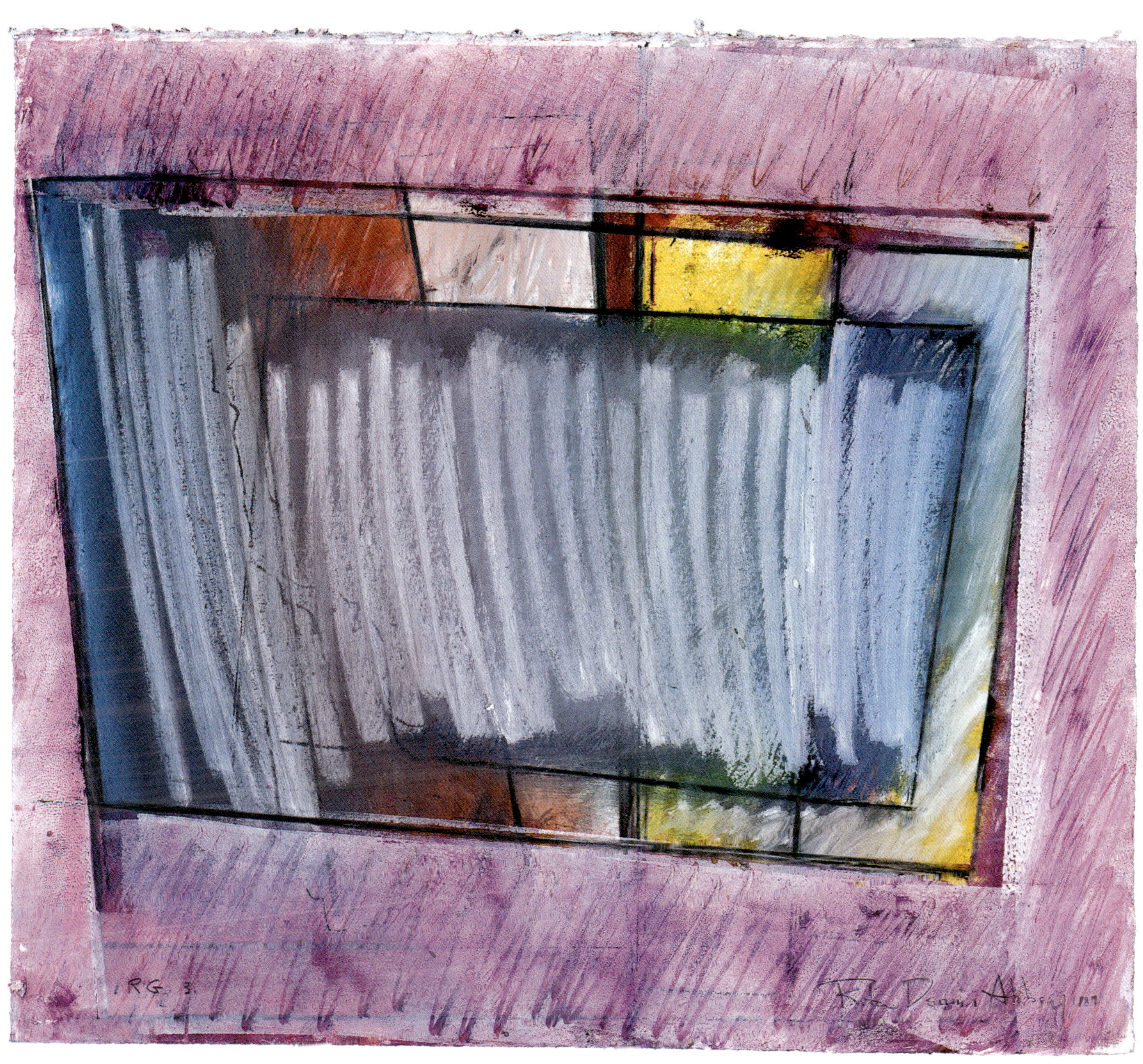

Rio Grande Series #4

Mixed media monotype on Rives BFK paper
13 1/4 x 15 inches

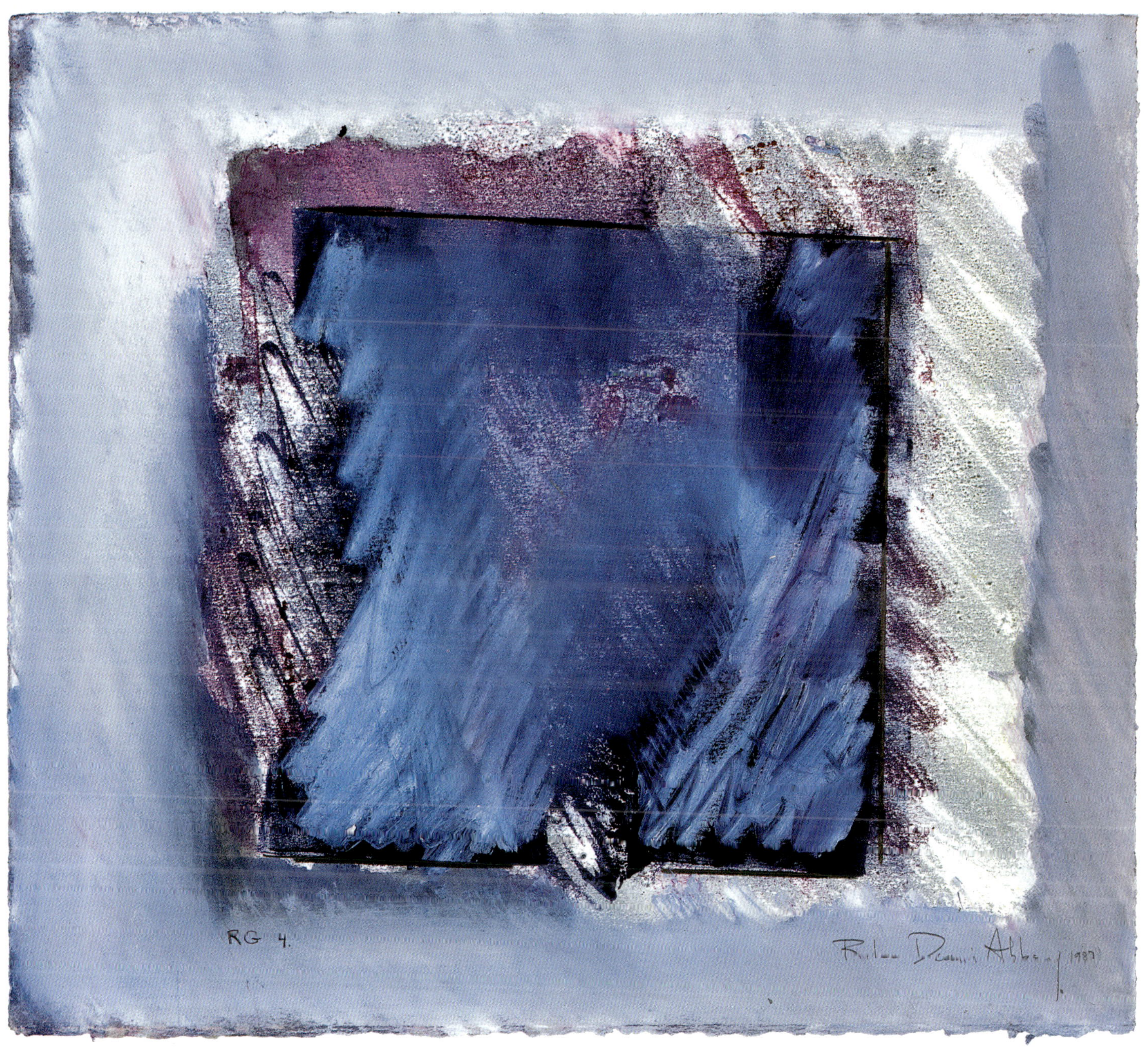
RG 4.

Rio Grande Series #5

Mixed media monotype on Rives BFK paper
13 1/8 x 15 1/4 inches

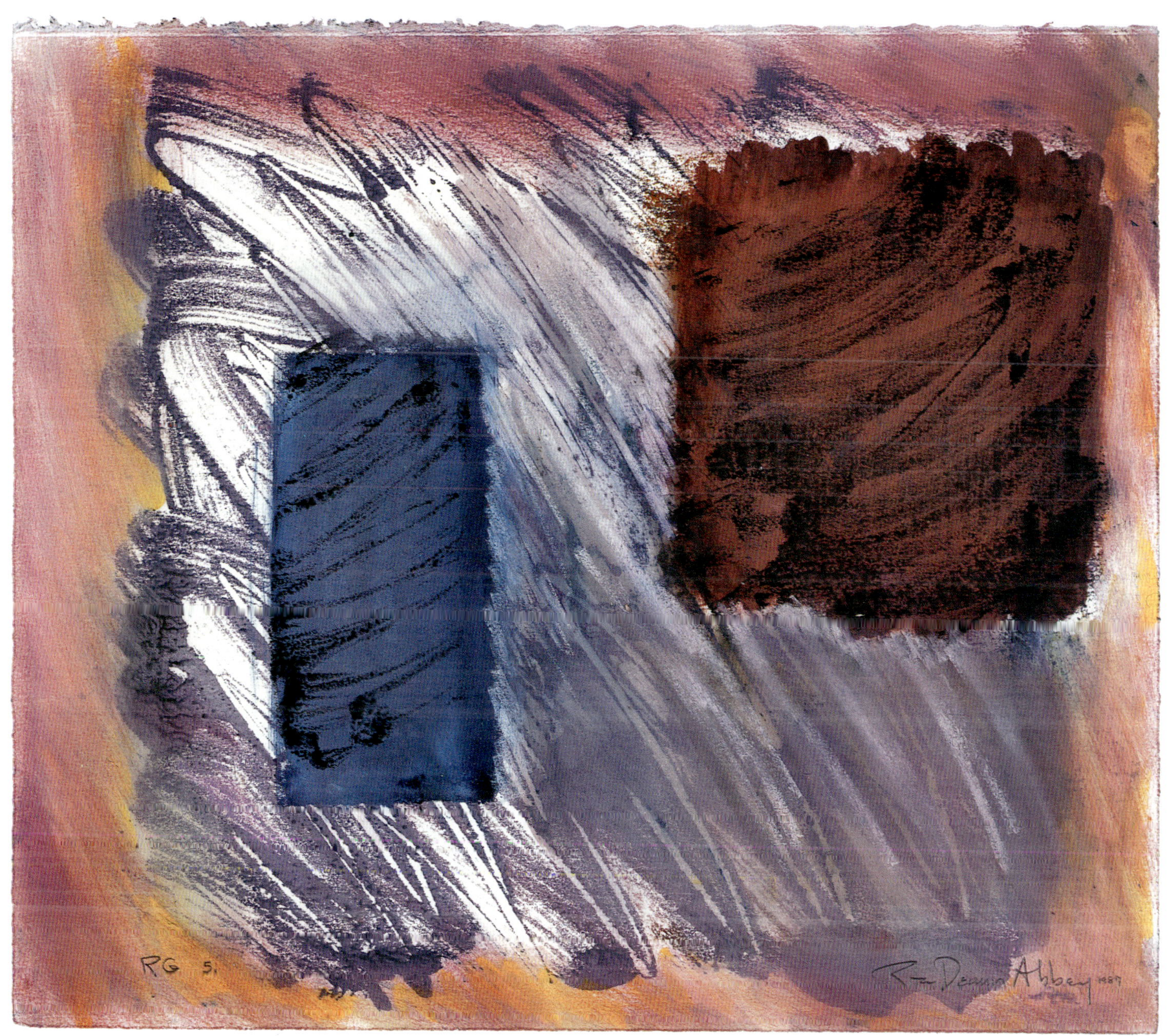

RIO GRANDE SERIES #6

Mixed media monotype on Rives BFK paper
13 x 15 inches

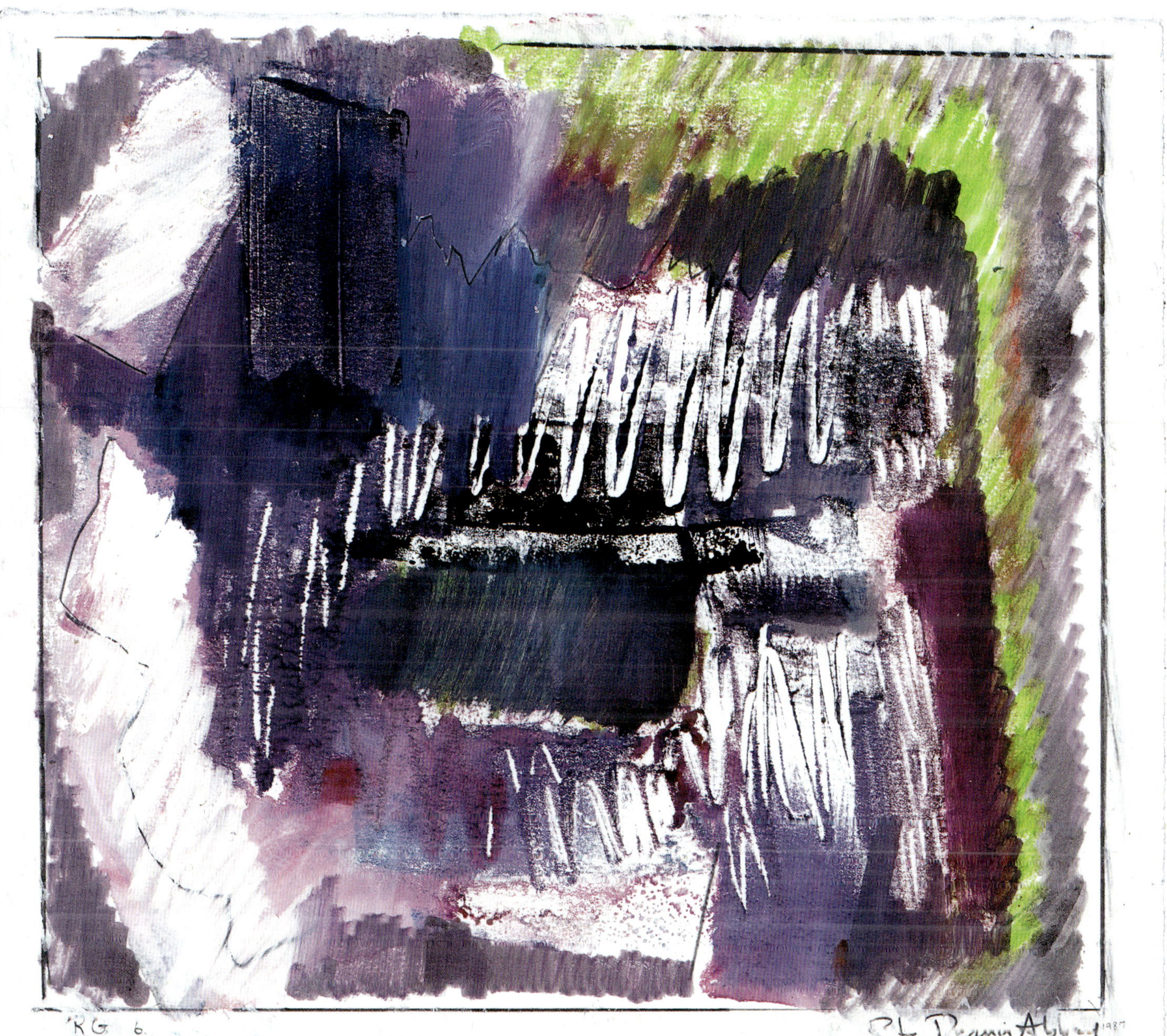

Rio Grande Series #7

Mixed media monotype on Rives BFK paper
13 x 15 1/4 inches

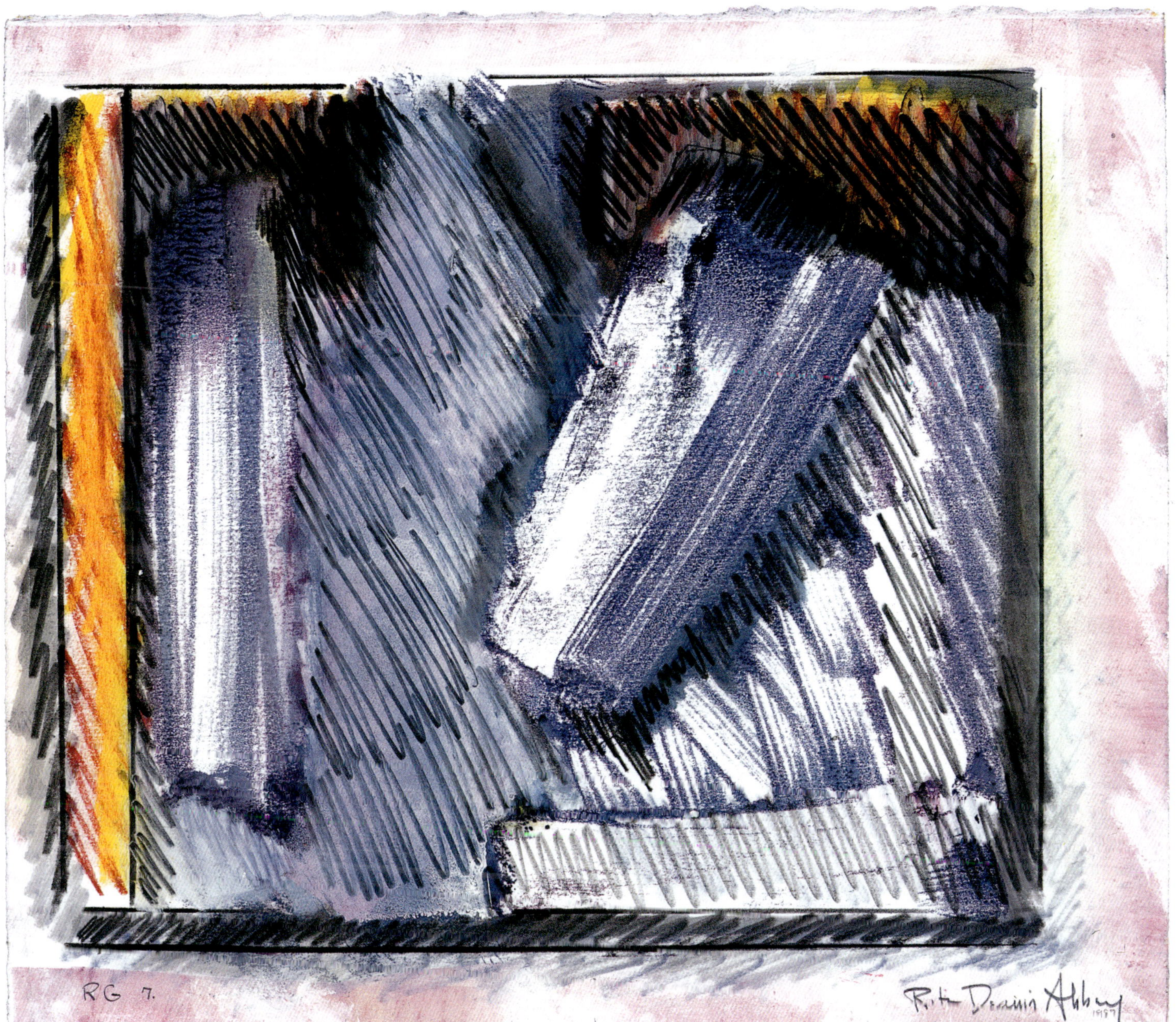

Rio Grande Series #8

Mixed media monotype on Rives BFK paper
13 x 15 1/4 inches

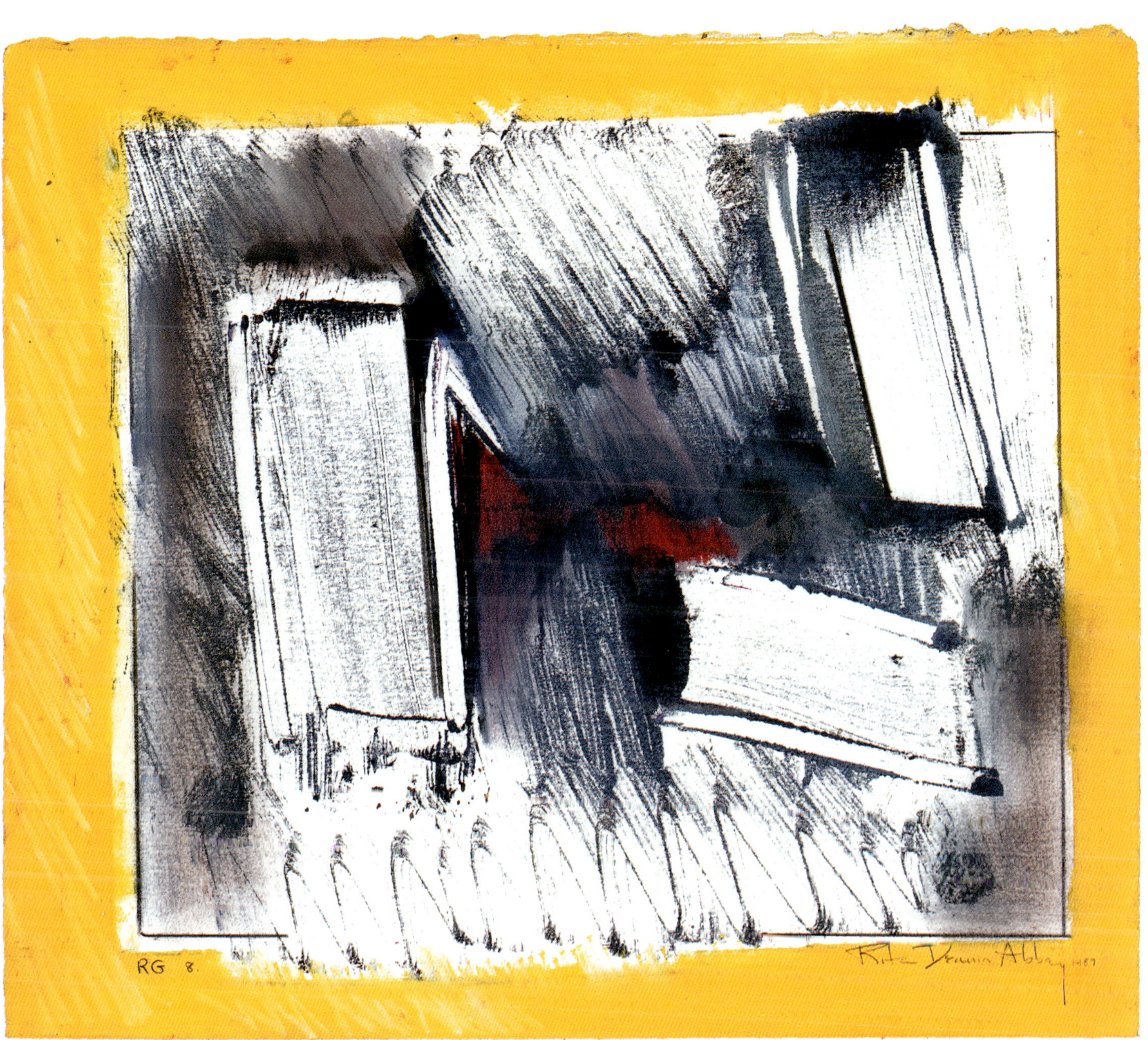
RG 8.

Rio Grande Series #9

Mixed media monotype on Rives BFK paper
13 1/4 x 15 inches

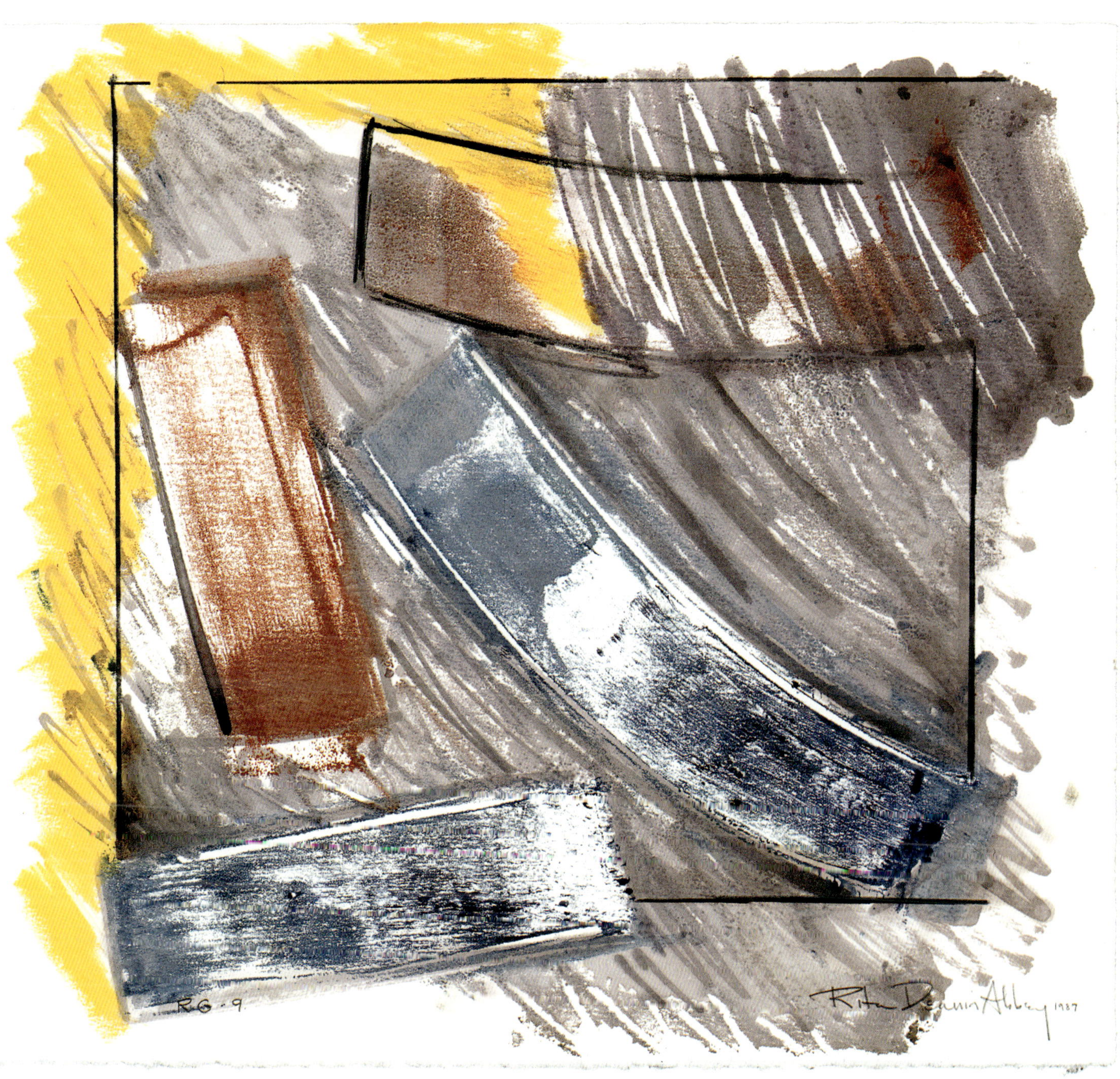
RG-9
Rita Deanin Abbey 1987

Rio Grande Series #10

Mixed media monotype on Rives BFK paper
$13\frac{1}{4}$ x 15 inches

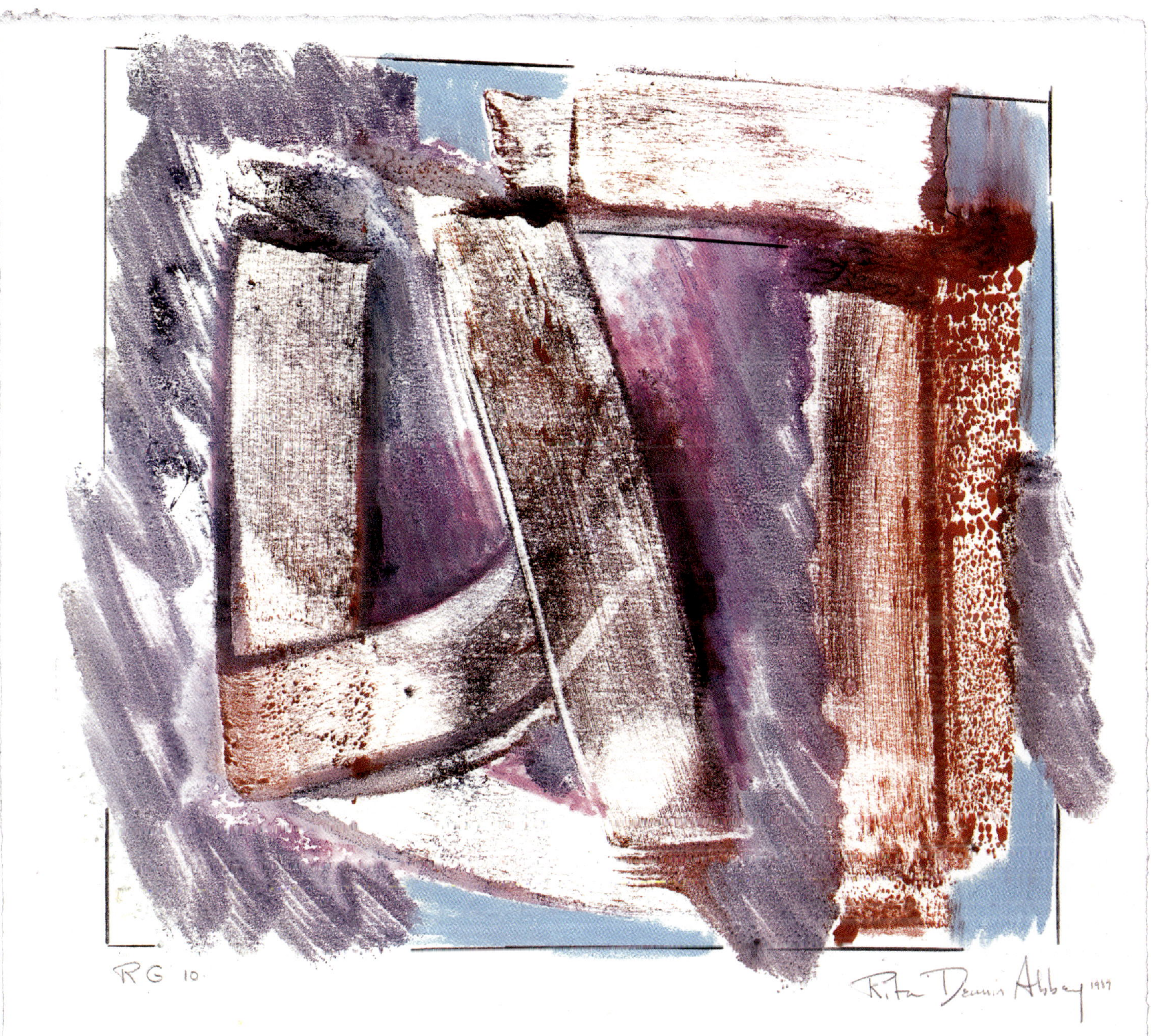

RIO GRANDE SERIES #11

Mixed media monotype on Rives BFK paper
13 1/4 x 15 1/4 inches

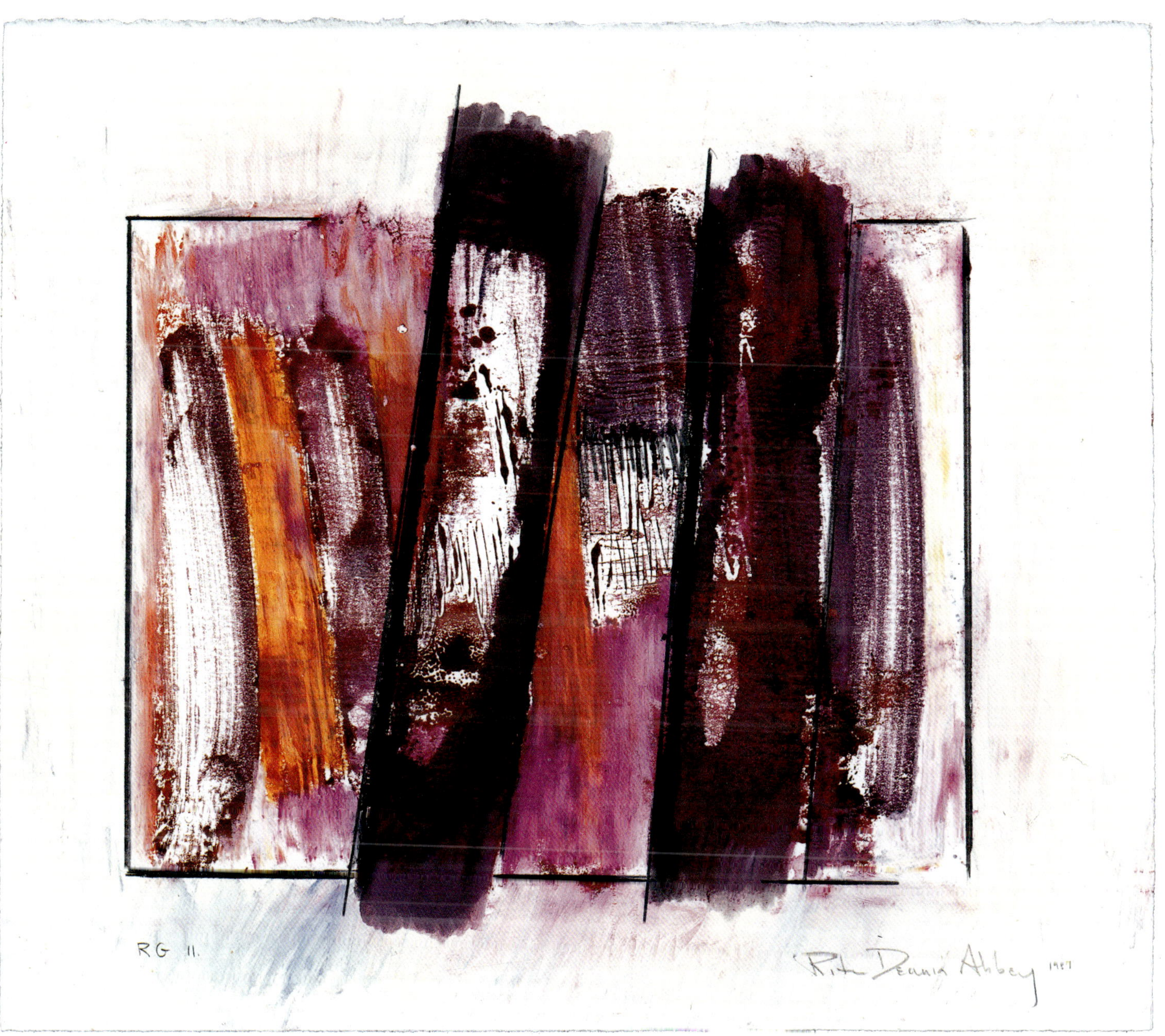
RG II.

Rio Grande Series #12

Mixed media monotype on Rives BFK paper
$13\frac{1}{4}$ x 15 inches

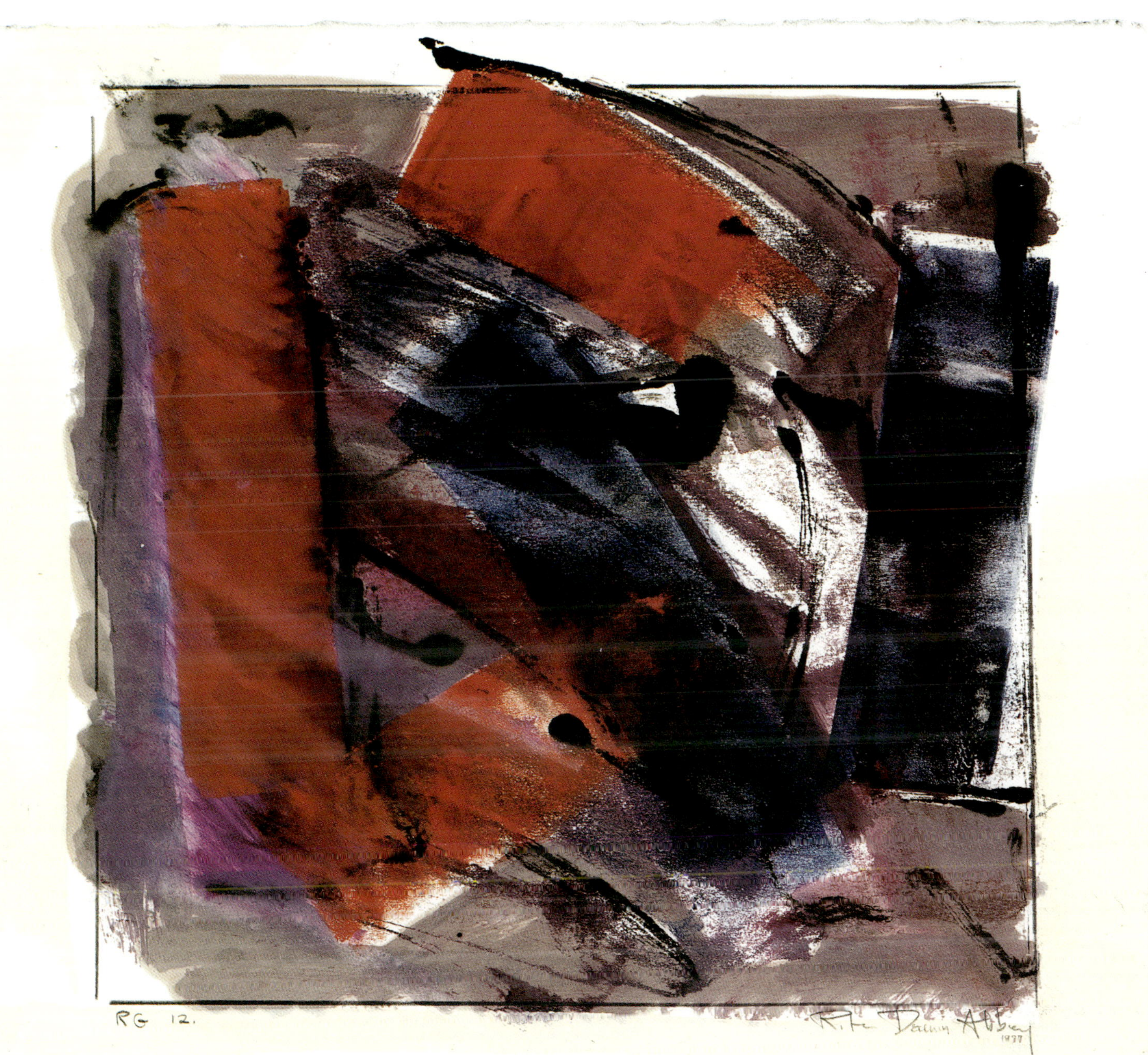
RG 12.

Rio Grande Series #13

Mixed media monotype on Rives BFK paper
13 1/4 x 15 inches

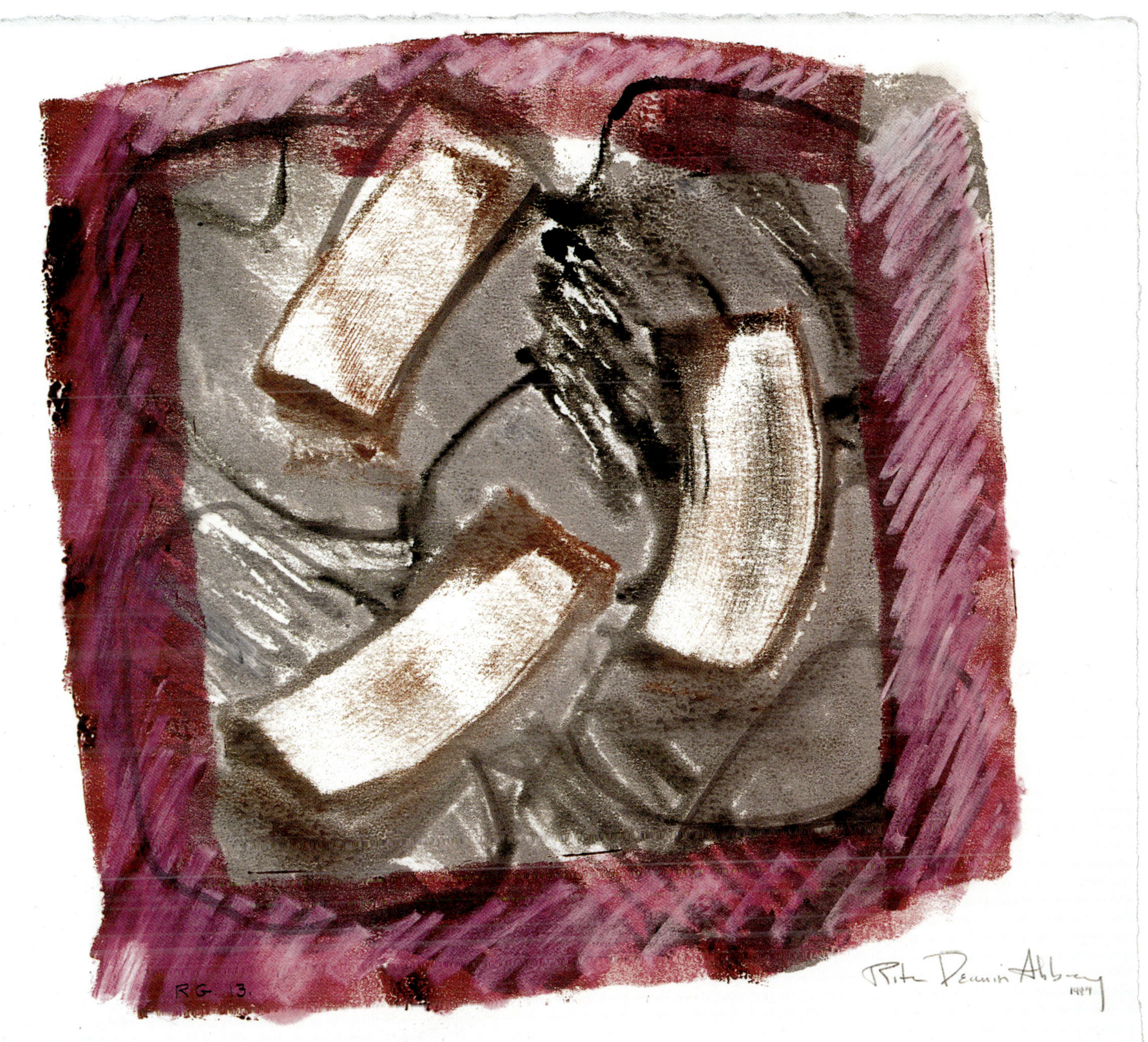
RG. 13.

RIO GRANDE SERIES #14

Mixed media monotype on Rives BFK paper
13¼ x 15¼ inches

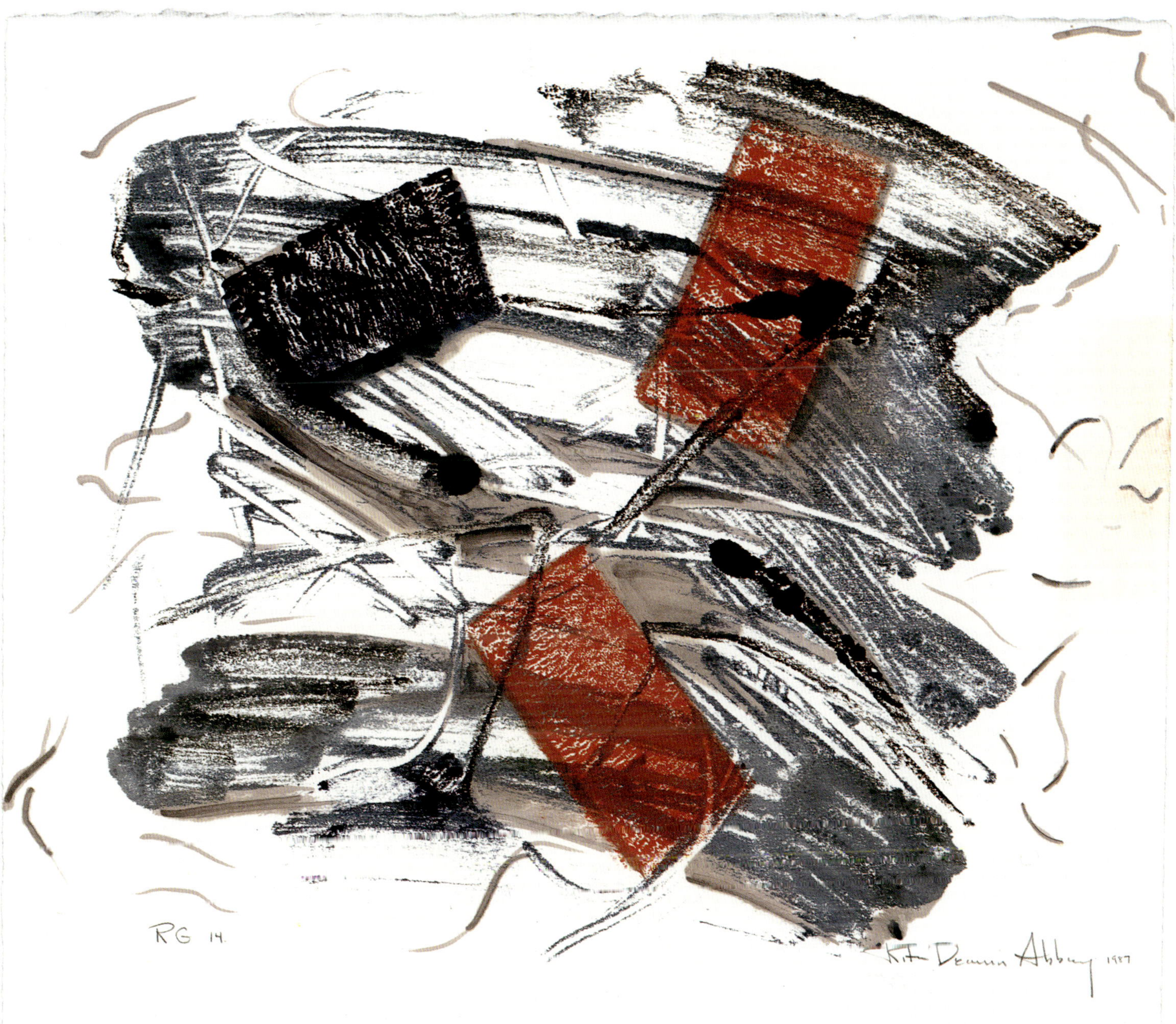
RG 14.
1987

Rio Grande Series #15

Mixed media monotype on Rives BFK paper
13 1/4 x 15 inches

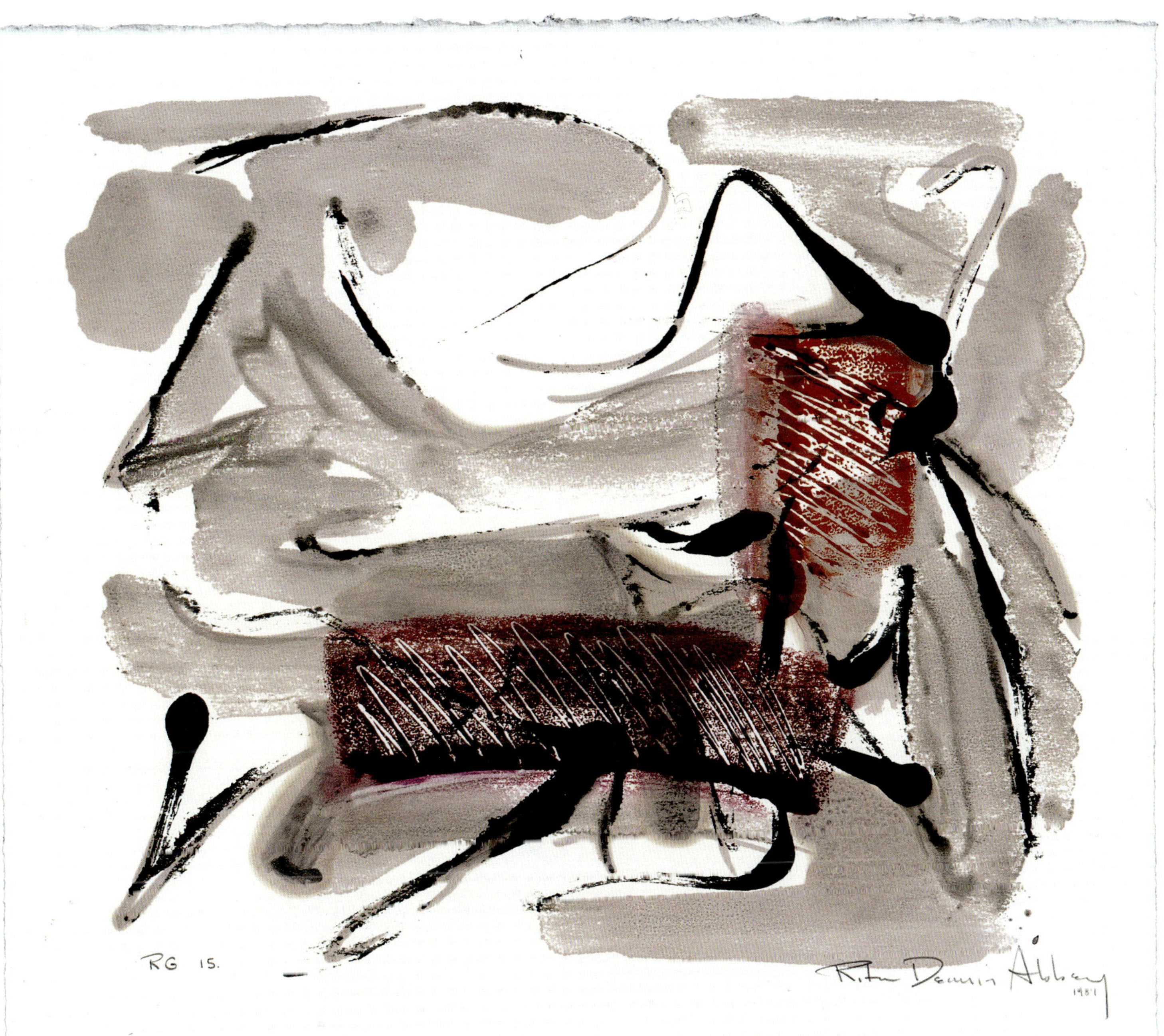
RG 15.
1981

Rio Grande Series #16

Mixed media monotype on Rives BFK paper
15 1/4 x 13 1/4 inches

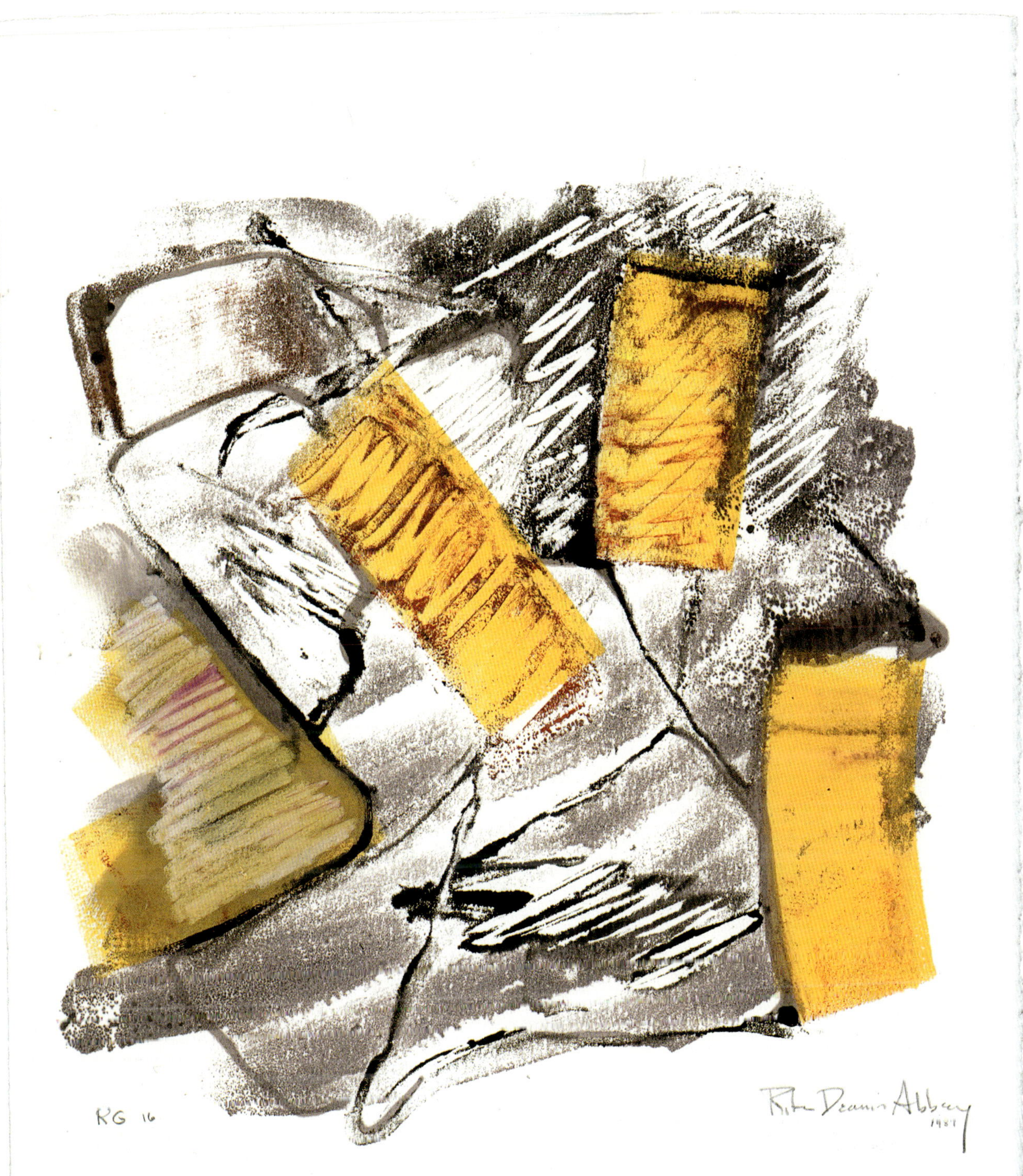
RG 16
Rita Deanin Abbey
1987

Rio Grande Series #17

Mixed media monotype on Rives BFK paper
13 1/4 x 15 1/4 inches

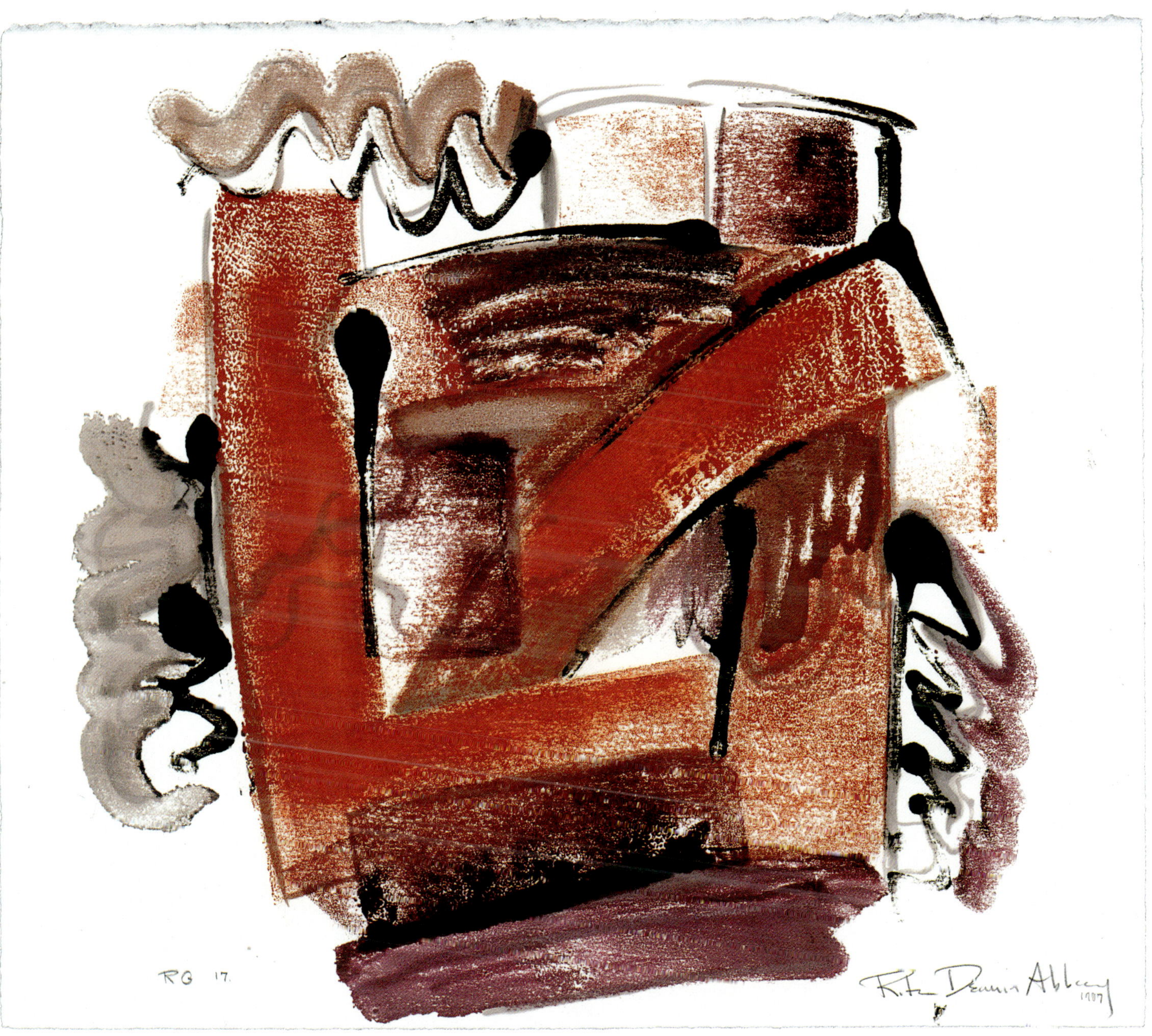

Rio Grande Series #18

Mixed media monotype on Rives BFK paper
includes Japanese papers of varying weights
13 1/4 x 15 inches

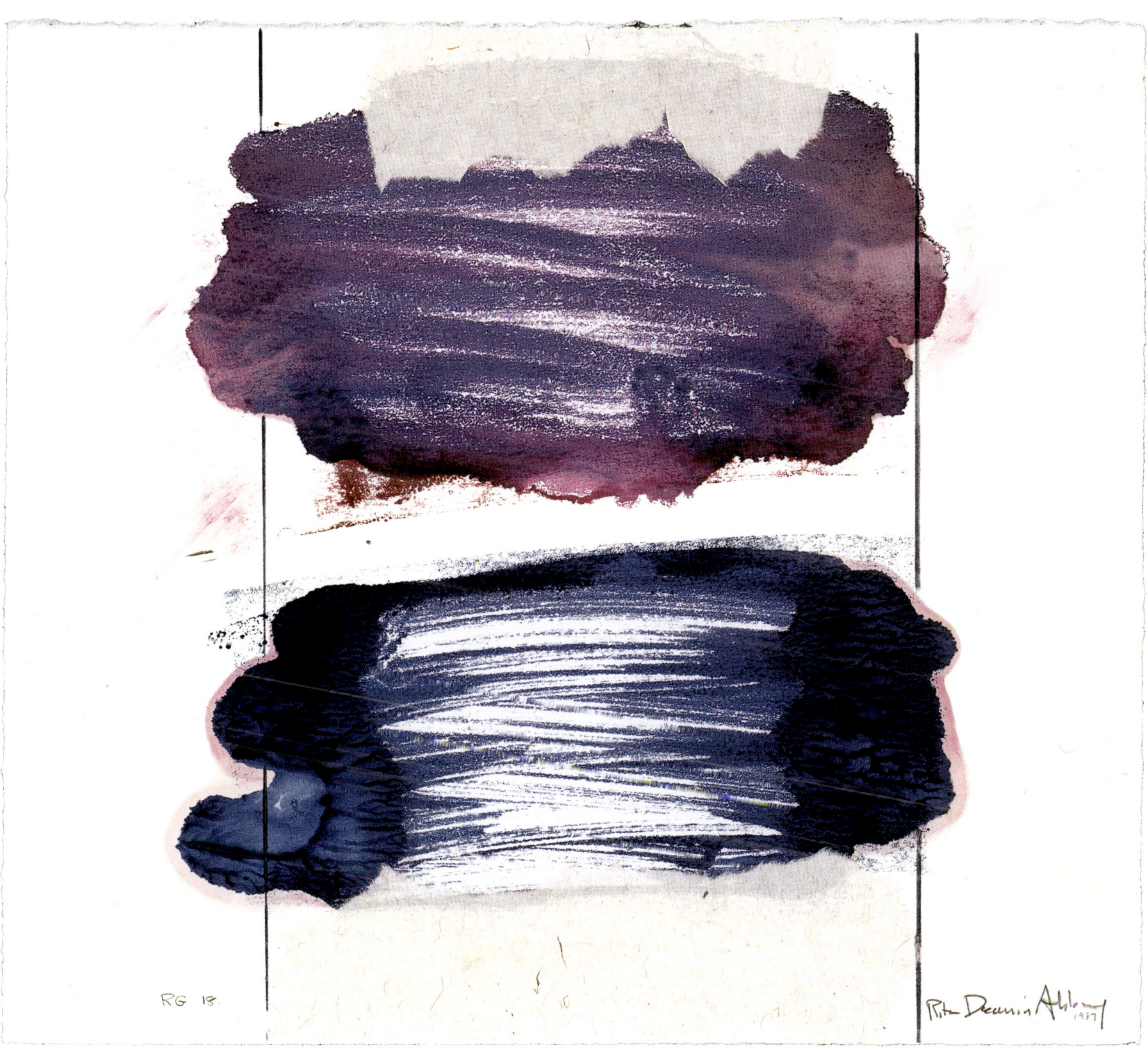

Rio Grande Series #19

Mixed media monotype on Rives BFK paper
13 1/4 x 15 inches

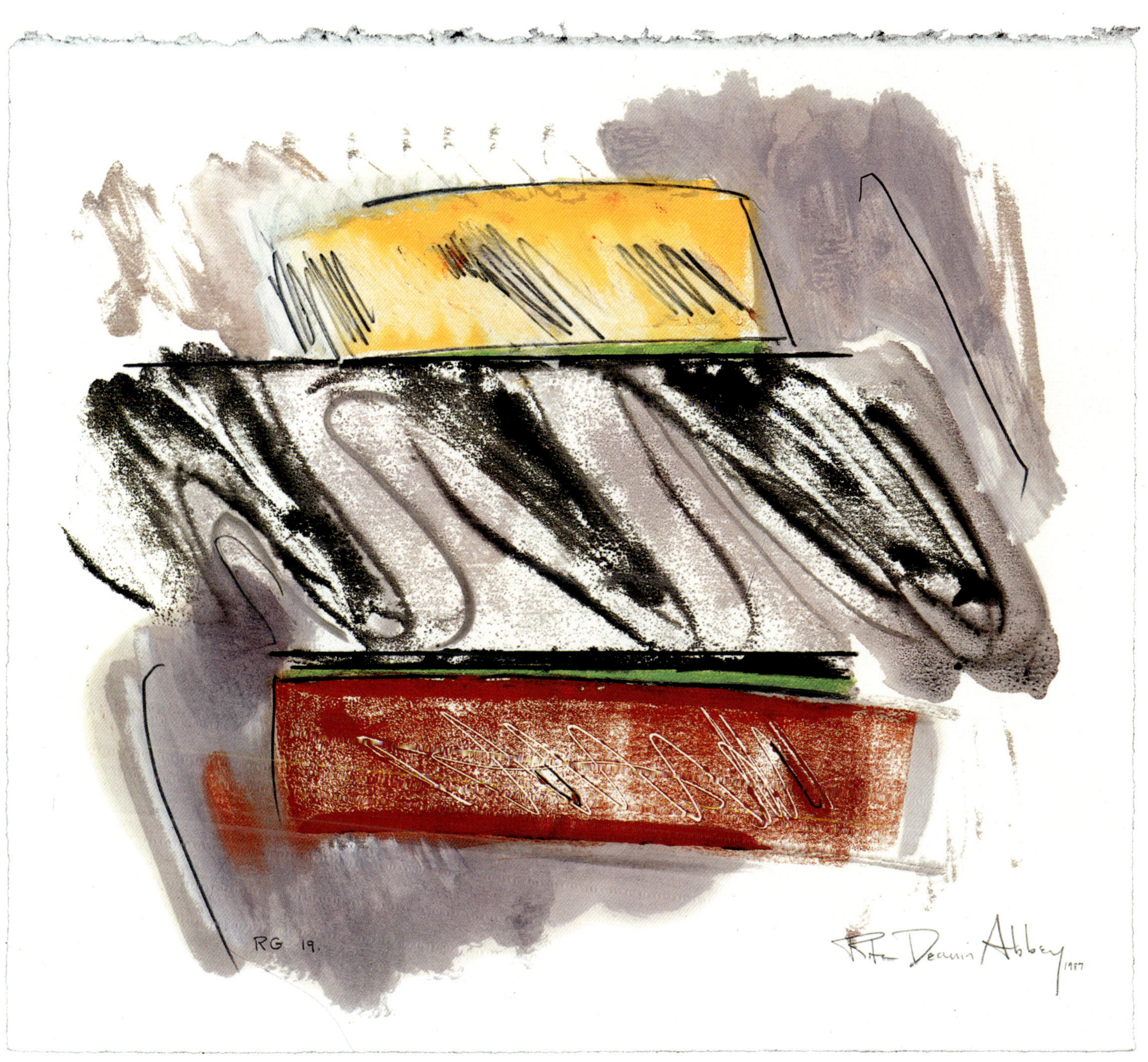
RG 19.
Rita Deanin Abbey 1987

Rio Grande Series #20

Mixed media monotype on Rives BFK paper
includes Japanese papers of varying weights
13 x 15 1/4 inches

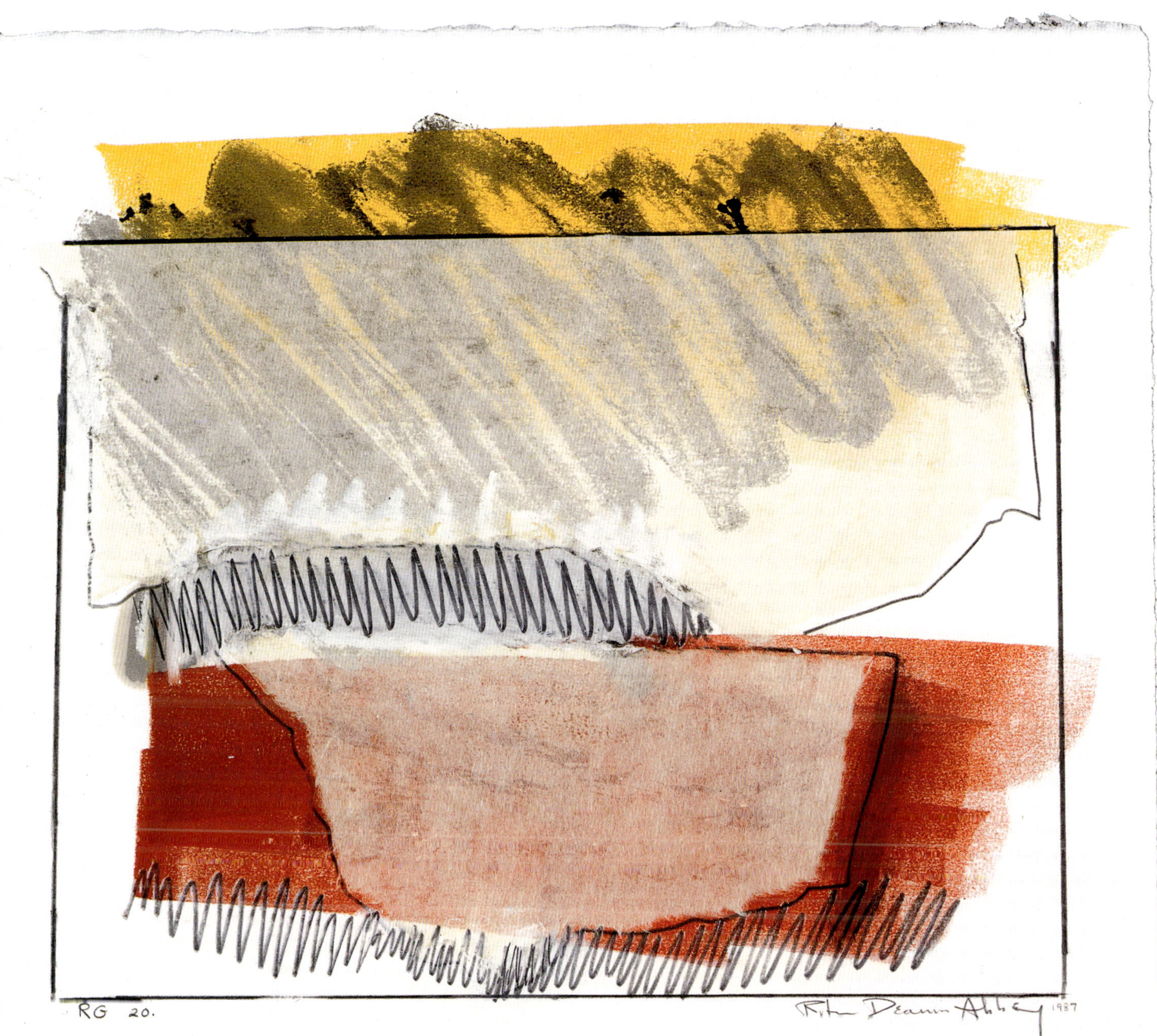
RG 20.
1987

Rio Grande Series #21

Mixed media monotype on Rives BFK paper
includes Japanese papers of varying weights
13 x 15 1/4 inches

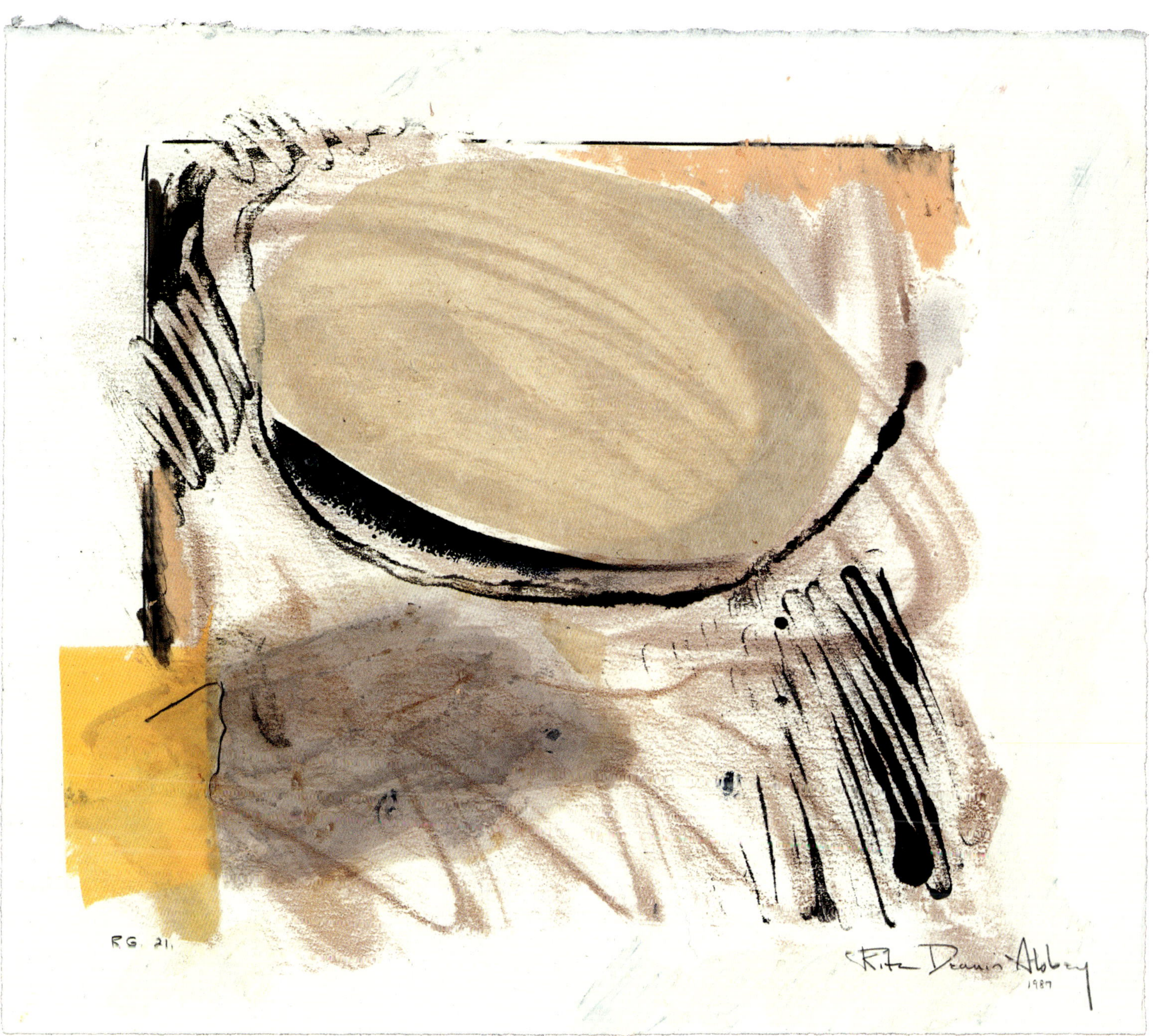

R.G. 21.
1987

Rio Grande Series #22

Mixed media monotype on Rives BFK paper
includes Japanese papers of varying weights
$13\frac{1}{4}$ x 15 inches

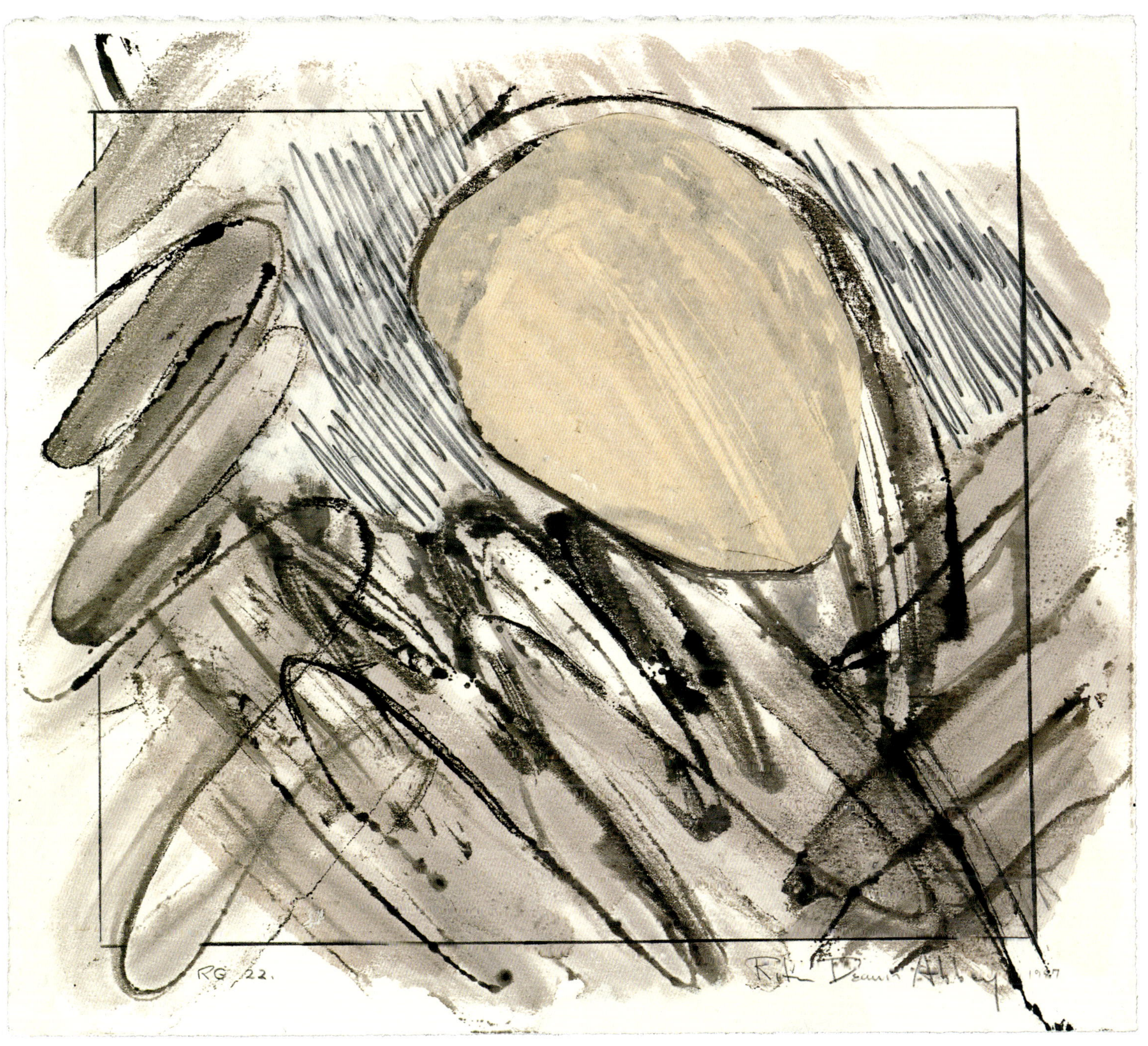

Rio Grande Series #23

Mixed media monotype on Rives BFK paper
13 1/4 x 15 1/4 inches

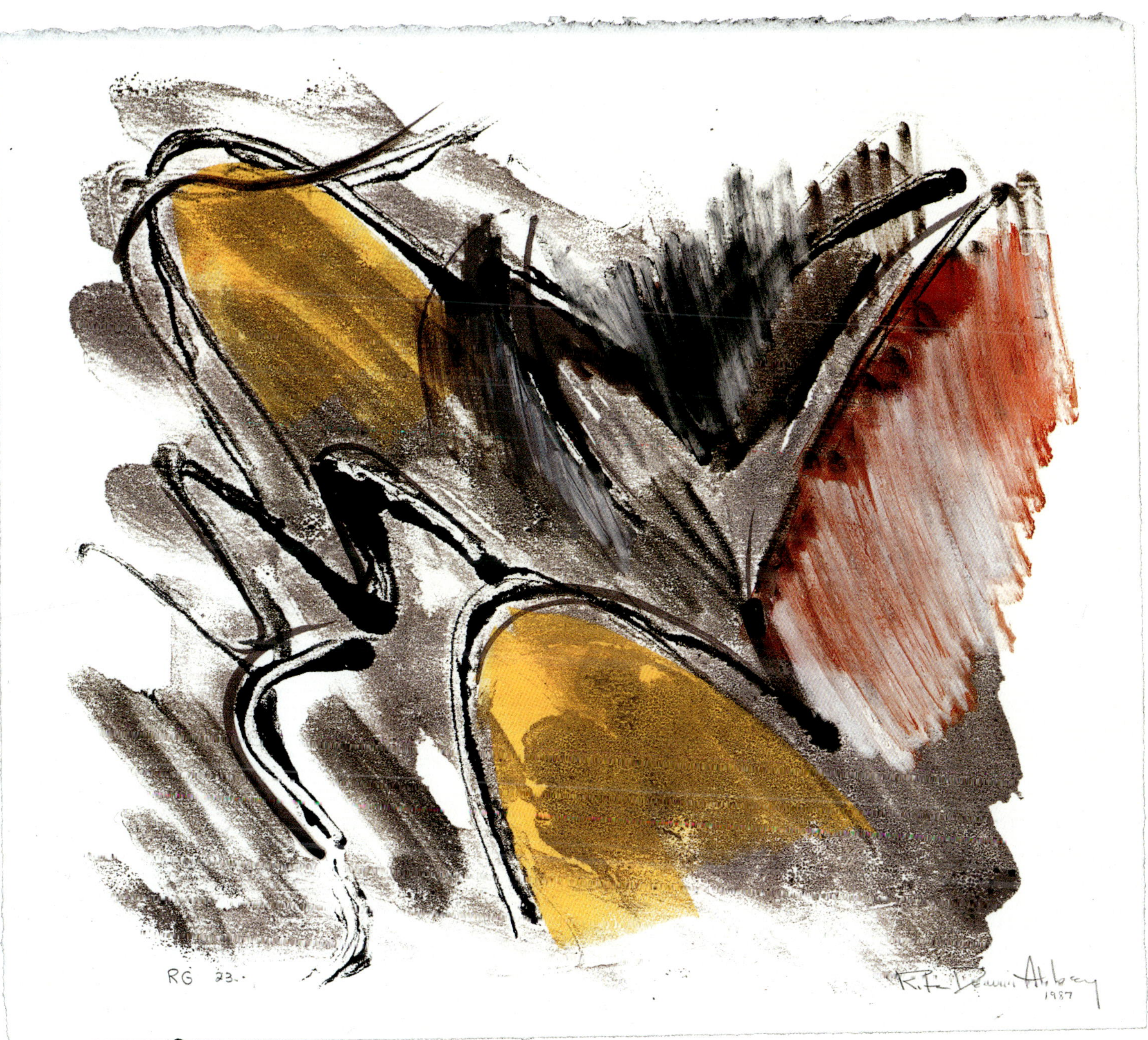

Rio Grande Series #24

Mixed media monotype on Rives BFK paper
13 1/4 x 15 1/4 inches

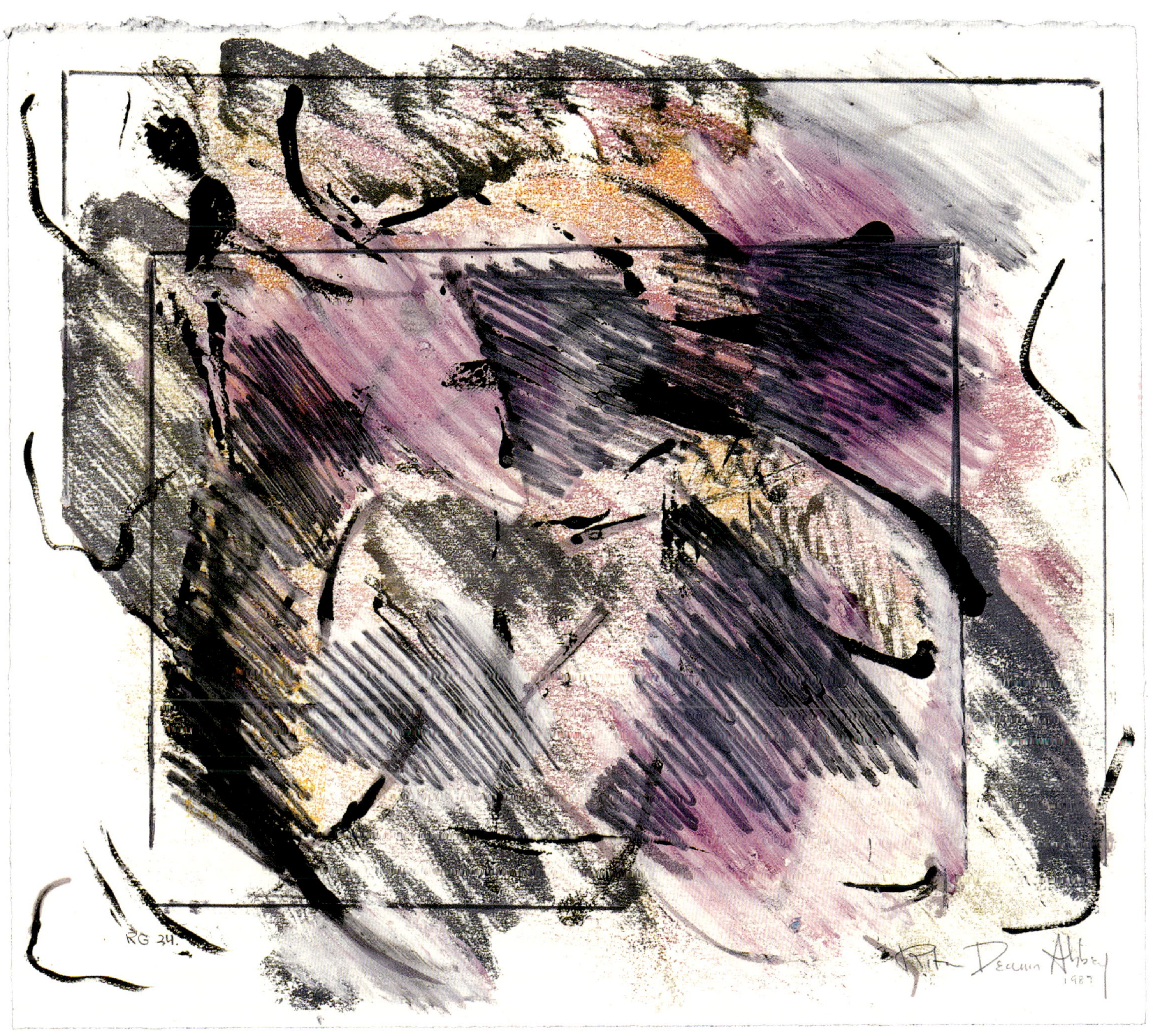
RG 24.
Rita Deanin Abbey
1987

Rio Grande Series #25

Mixed media monotype on Rives BFK paper includes Japanese papers of varying weights
13 1/4 x 15 1/4 inches

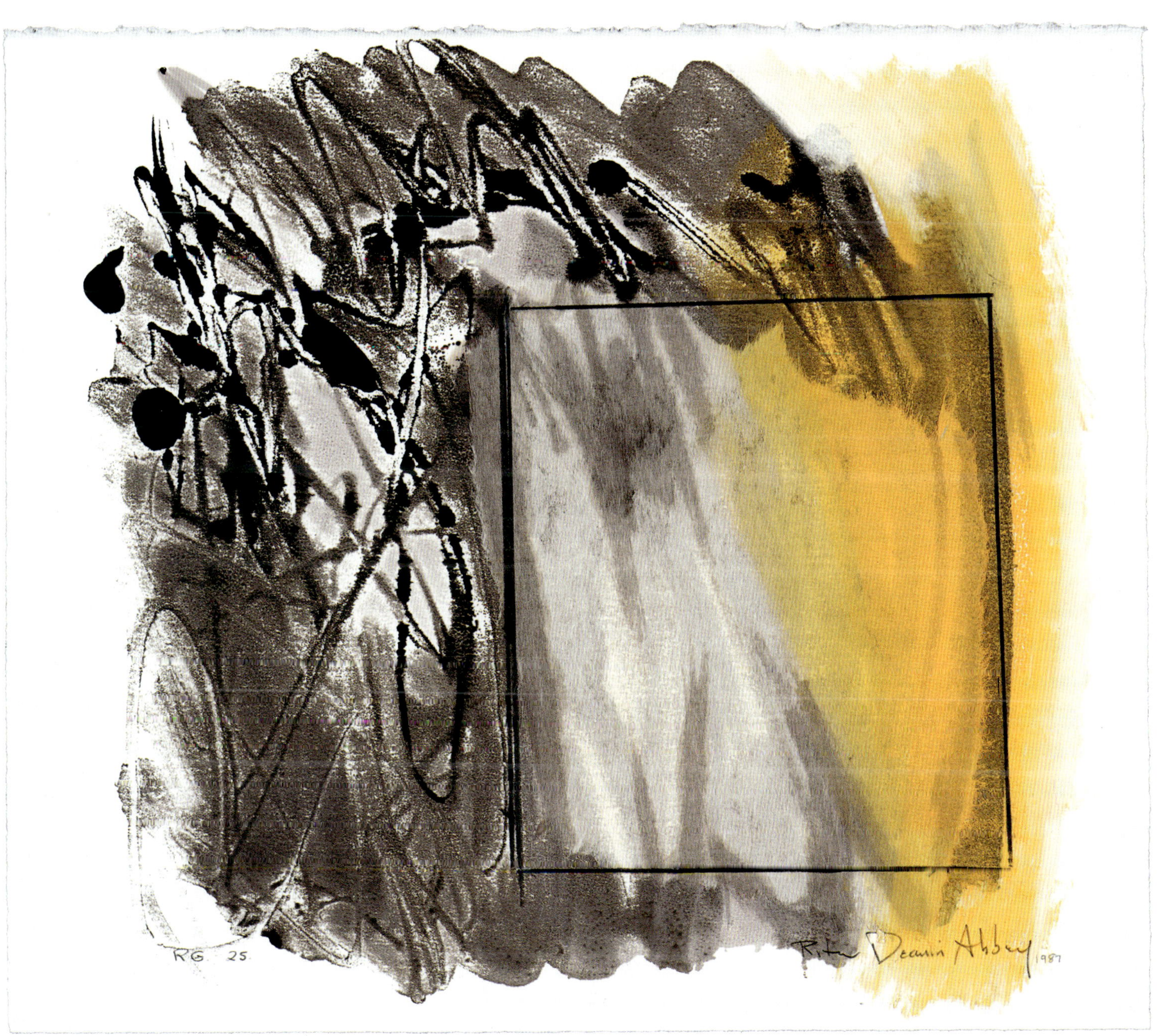
RG. 25
Rita Deanin Abbey 1987

Rio Grande Series #26

Mixed media monotype on Rives BFK paper includes Japanese papers of varying weights
13 1/4 x 15 1/4 inches

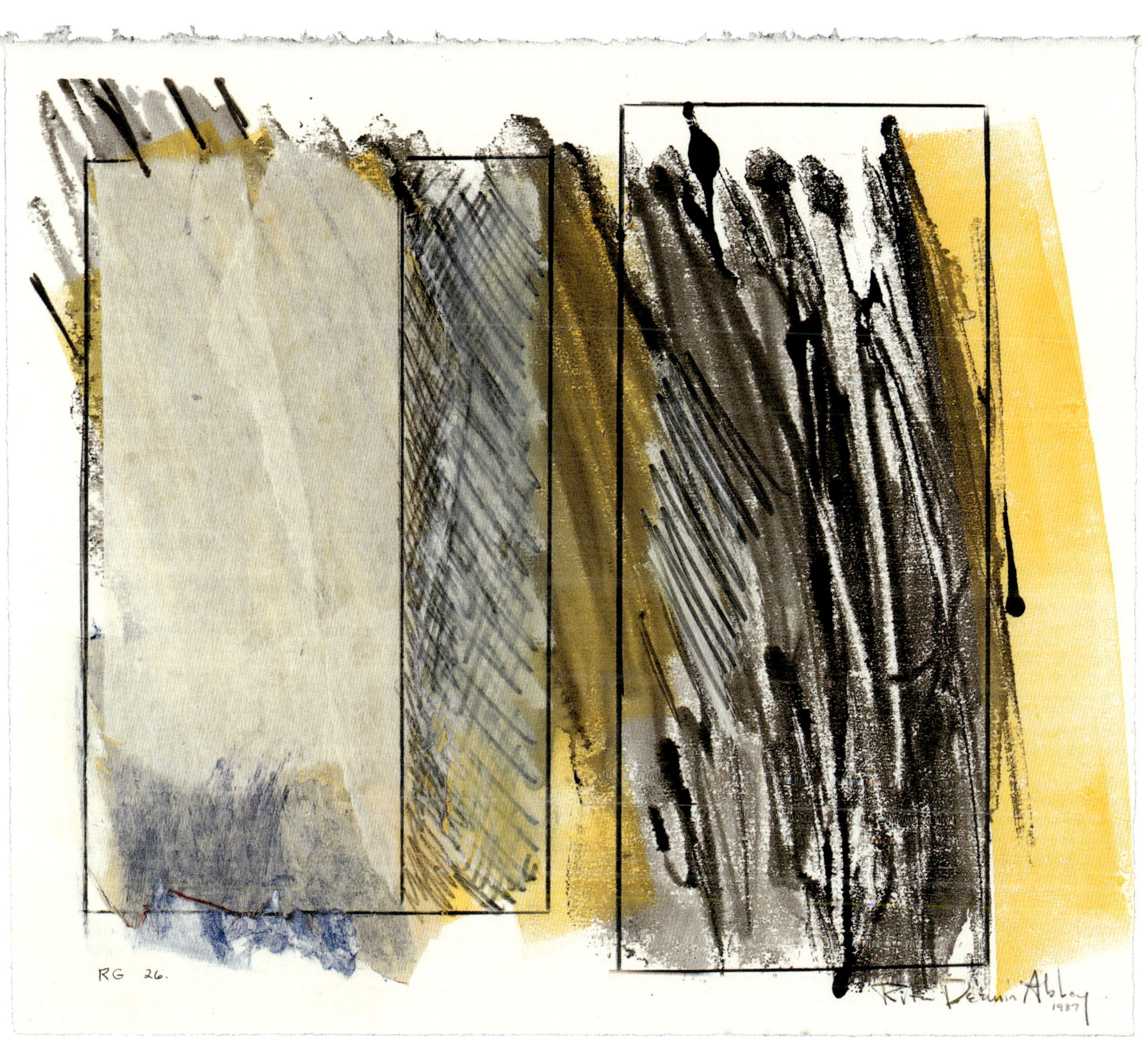
RG 26.
1987

Rio Grande Series #27

Mixed media monotype on Rives BFK paper
13 1/4 x 15 inches

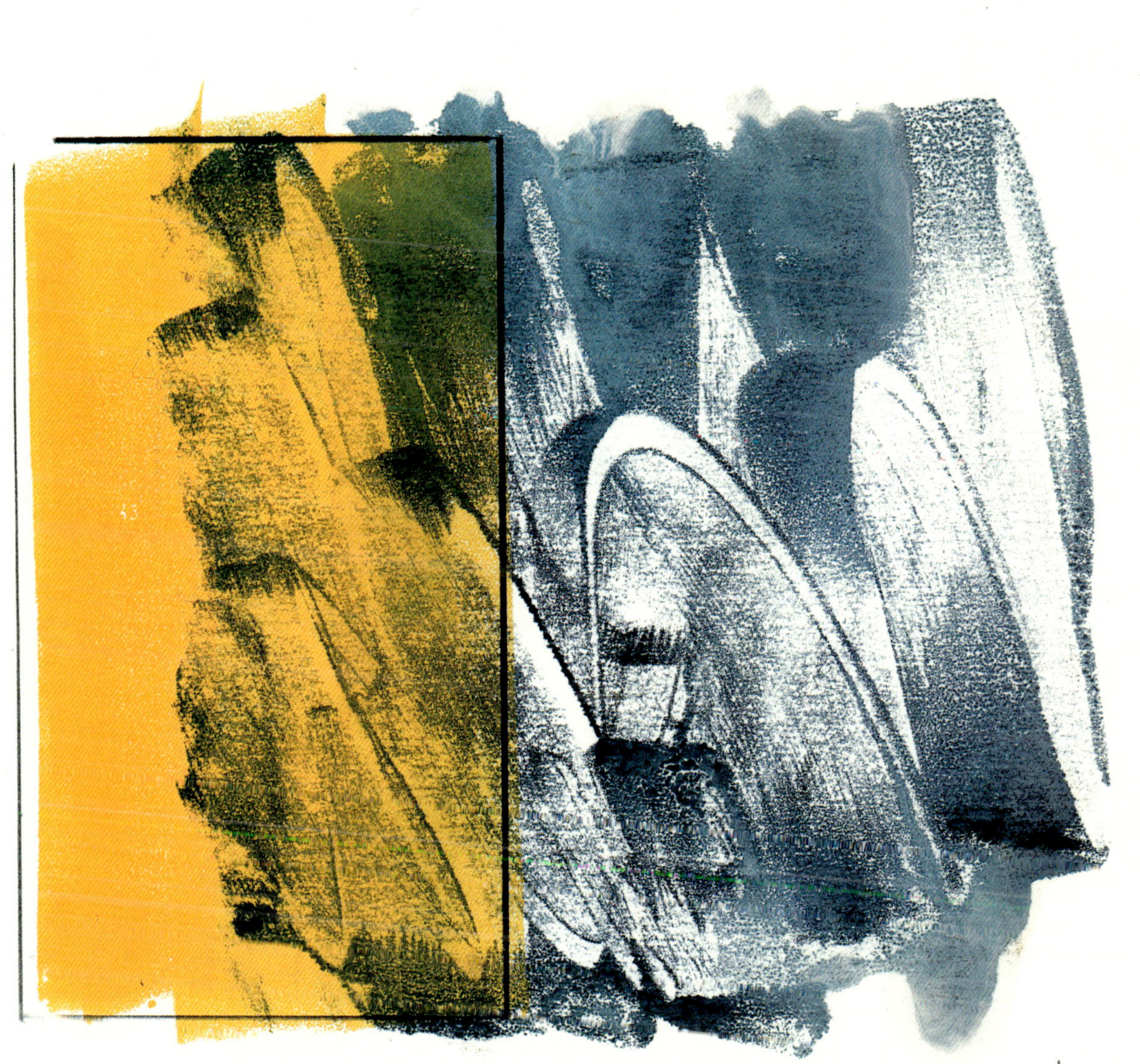

RG 27
Rita Deanin Abbey
1987

Rio Grande Series #28

Mixed media monotype on Rives BFK paper
includes Japanese papers of varying weights
$13\frac{1}{4}$ x $15\frac{1}{4}$ inches

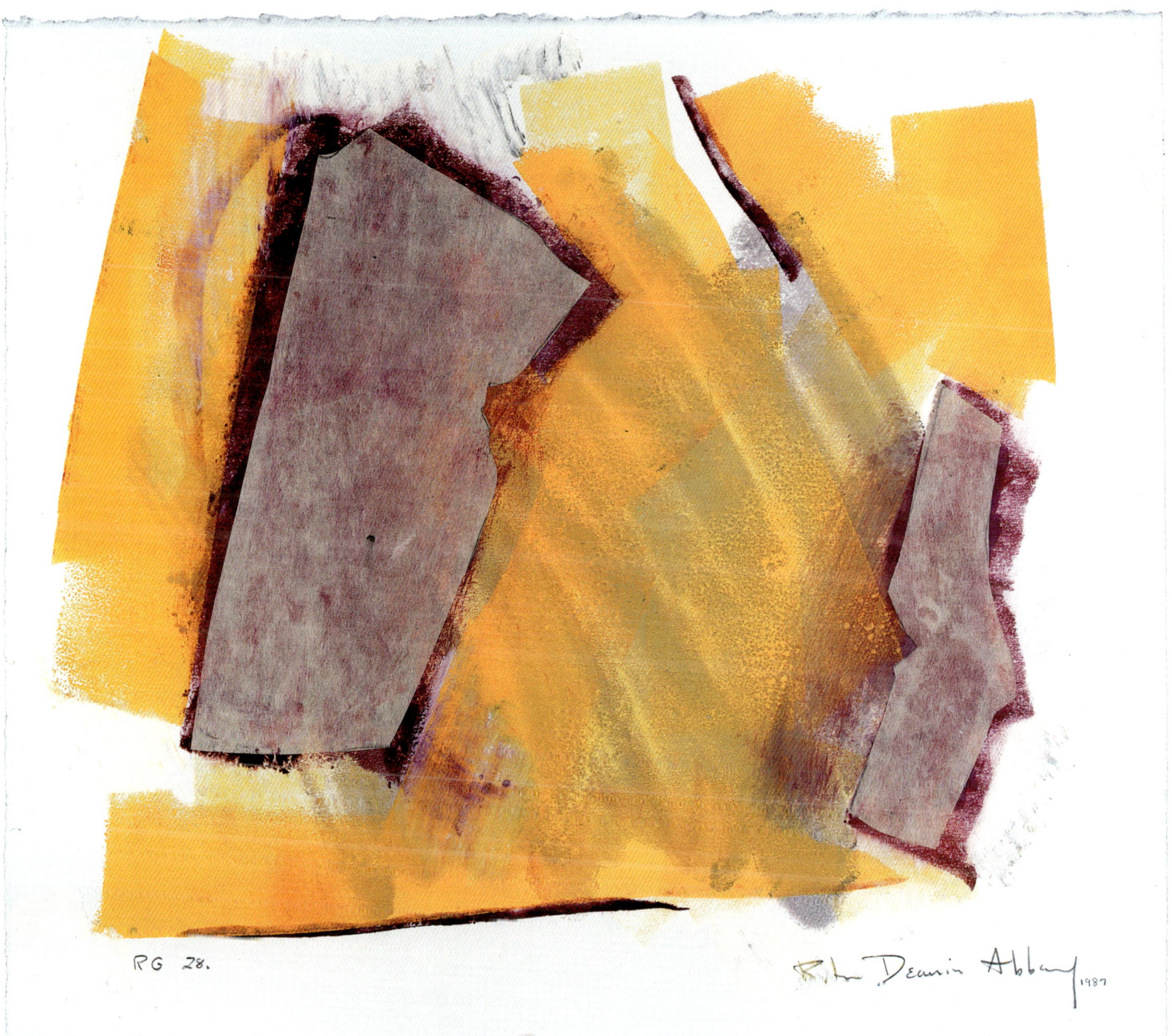
RG 28.
1987

Rio Grande Series #29

Mixed media monotype on Rives BFK paper includes Japanese papers of varying weights
13 1/4 x 15 inches

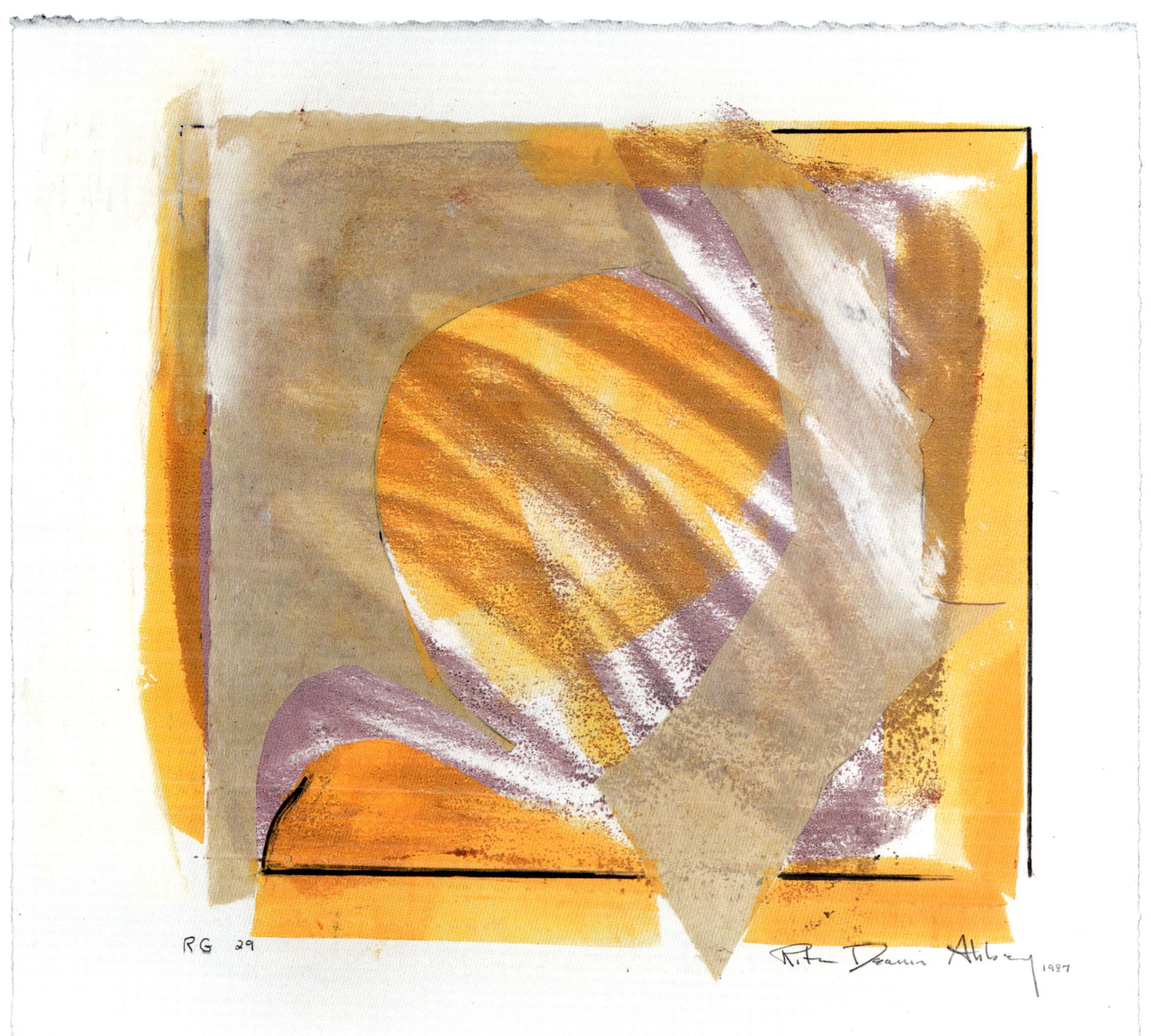
RG 29
1987

Rio Grande Series #30

Mixed media monotype on Rives BFK paper
includes Japanese papers of varying weights
$13\,^1/_4$ x $15\,^1/_4$ inches

Rio Grande Series #31

Mixed media monotype on Rives BFK paper
includes Japanese papers of varying weights
13 1/4 x 15 1/4 inches

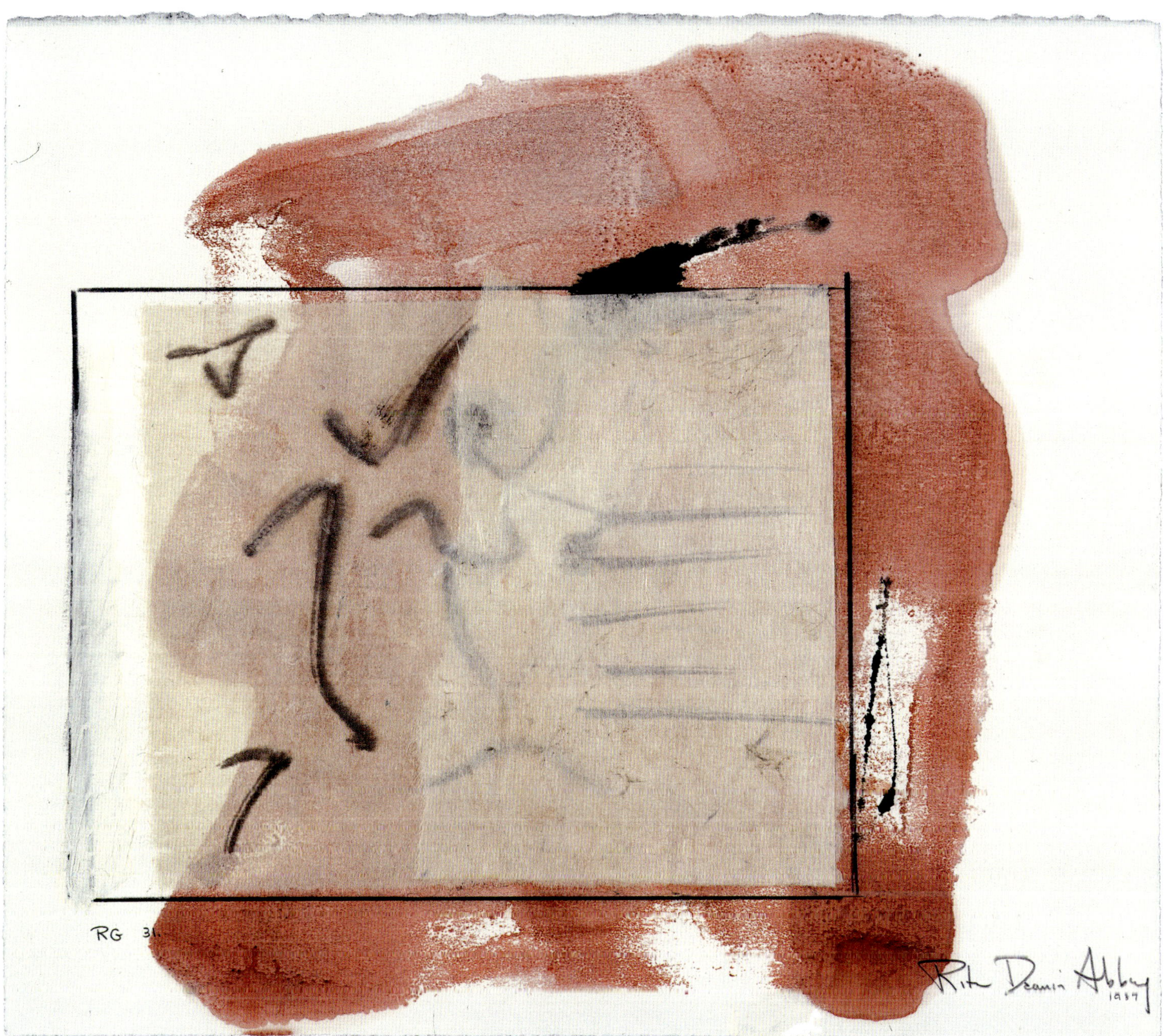
RG 31
Rita Deanin Abbey
1987

Rio Grande Series #32

Mixed media monotype on Rives BFK paper includes Japanese papers of varying weights
13 1/4 x 15 inches

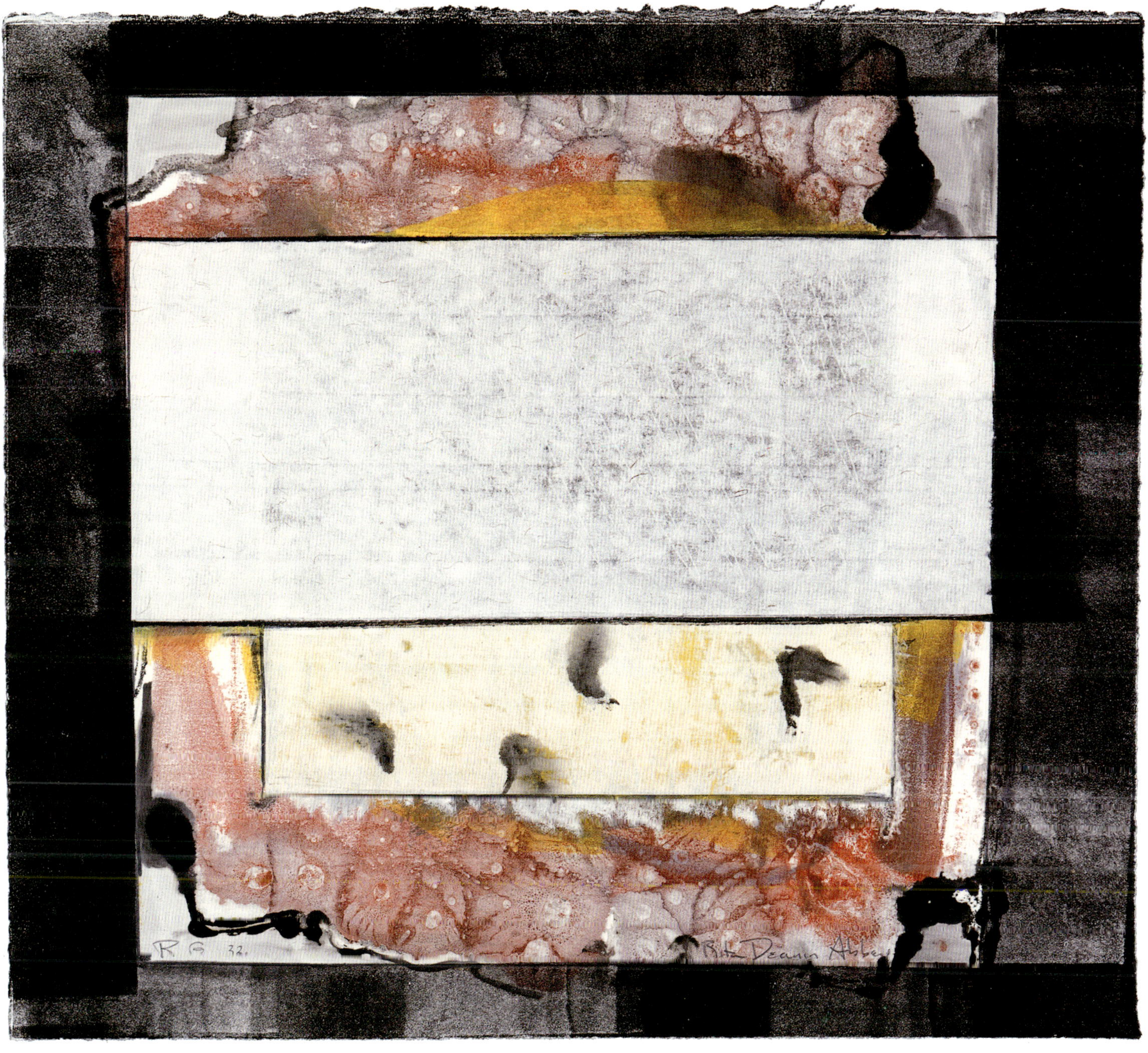

Artist's Biography

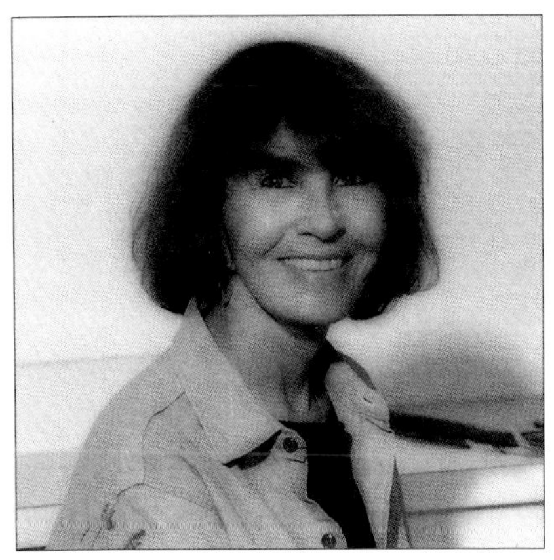

Rita Deanin Abbey is an Emeritus Professor of Art at the University of Nevada, Las Vegas. She taught drawing, painting, and color theory at UNLV from 1965 to 1987. The University of Nevada, Las Vegas, Marjorie Barrick Museum and the Palm Springs Desert Museum, Palm Springs, CA collaborated to present the *Rita Deanin Abbey 35 Year Retrospective,* which was held February 16–March 5, 1988 at UNLV and March 25–June 5, 1988 at the Palm Springs Desert Museum.

Abbey received her Bachelor of Fine Arts degree in 1952 and her Master of Arts degree in 1954 from the University of New Mexico, Albuquerque, NM. She also studied at Goddard College, Plainfield, VT; the Art Student's League, Woodstock, NY; the Hans Hofmann School of Fine Arts, Provincetown, MA; and the San Francisco Art Institute, San Francisco, CA. She was an artist in residence in the studios of Toshi Yoshida, Tokyo, Japan; John Killmaster, Boise, ID; Methow Iron Works, Twisp, WA; Tamarind Institute, University of New Mexico, Albuquerque, NM, the Mason Gross School of the Arts, Rutgers, The State University of New Jersey, New Brunswick, NJ; and Shidoni Foundry, Tesuque, NM.

Abbey, who works in the areas of painting, drawing, printmaking, sculpture, porcelain enamel fired on steel, and computer art, has had 50 individual exhibitions and has participated in over 100 national and international group exhibitions. She is represented in many private and public collections in the United States and Europe.

Abbey has published several articles in journals, and two books: *Rivertrip,* Northland Press, Flagstaff, AZ, 1977, and *Art and Geology: Expressive Aspects of the Desert,* Peregrine Smith Books, Layton, UT, 1986 (co-authored by G. William Fiero). She has been the recipient of many commissions and grants and has won several awards, including the Bicentennial Commission for the State of Nevada, 1976; the Governor's Seventh Annual Visual Arts Award for the State of Nevada, 1986; and the Chairman's Award of Excellence at the *1987 International Exhibition of Enamelling Art in Japan,* Ueno Royal Museum, Tokyo. Abbey was invited by the Gallery Association of New York State to exhibit four of her works in its 1989–1991 traveling exhibition, *Color and Image: Recent American Enamels.* In 1992, the Markus Galleries, Las Vegas, NV, and the Nevada Symphony presented an exhibition of art by Abbey which inspired Virko Baley's *Piano Concerto No. 1.* The world premiere performance of the concerto was held in 1993 at the National Opera House, Kiev, Ukraine. Also in 1993, Abbey constructed a 20 ft., cor-ten steel sculpture, *Spirit Tower,* which was commissioned by the Las Vegas-Clark County Library District for the Summerlin Library and Performing Arts Center. She was one of three artists from the United States invited to participate in the exhibition, *Enamel Today,* at Villa am Aabach, Uster, Switzerland, June–July, 1995. Abbey is currently working on a series of cast bronze sculptures. ■